SOUL ALCHEMY

Ascension Codes to Live a Life Beyond Your Wildest Dreams

HOUSE OF INDIGO

Contents

Disclaimer

The publisher and the authors are providing this book and its contents on an "as is" basis and make no representations or warranties of any kind with respect to this book or its contents. The publisher and the author disclaim all such representations and warranties, including but not limited to warranties of healthcare for a particular purpose.

In addition, the publisher and the author assume no responsibility for errors, inaccuracies, omissions, or any other inconsistencies herein.

The content of this book is for informational purposes only and is

not intended to diagnose, treat, cure, or prevent any condition or disease. You understand that this book is not intended as a substitute for consultation with a licensed practitioner. Please consult with your own physician or healthcare specialist regarding the suggestions and recommendations made in this book.

The use of this book implies your acceptance of this disclaimer.

Disclaimer

The publisher and the author make no guarantees concerning the level of success you may experience by following the advice and strategies contained in this book, and you accept the risk that results will differ for each individual. The testimonials and examples provided in this book show exceptional results, which may not apply to the average reader, and are not intended to represent or guarantee that you will achieve the same or similar results.

Introduction

Welcome to "Soul Alchemy: Ascension Codes to Live a Life Beyond Your Wildest Dreams," an anthology book that offers a transformative journey towards self-discovery, healing, and spiritual growth. This collection of insightful essays, personal stories, and practical tools is designed to help you unlock your true potential and live the life you've always dreamed of.

This book is accompanied by a powerful workbook that provides you with a step-by-step guide to applying the ascension codes outlined in the book to your own life. The combination of the anthology and workbook gives you access to a wealth of knowledge and techniques that will empower you to make positive changes and take control of your destiny.

Each chapter in this book is authored by a leader, practitioner, or coach sharing their unique perspective and experience on topics such as inner child healing, moon cycles, energy healing, and more. Whether you're new to spiritual practice or a seasoned seeker, this book offers a comprehensive and accessible resource for your spiritual journey.

We suggest using this book as a tool for personal reflection and growth. Take your time reading through each chapter, and use the accompanying workbook to dive deeper into the teachings and exercises presented. The workbook also includes journaling prompts, affirmations, and meditation practices that will help you integrate the lessons and concepts into your daily life.

"Soul Alchemy: Ascension Codes to Live a Life Beyond Your Wildest Dreams" is a guidebook for anyone who wants to transform their life from the inside out. It offers a roadmap for those seeking to align with their true purpose, release limiting beliefs, and tap into their infinite potential. Let this book be your companion on your journey toward a life of fulfillment, joy, and abundance.

ONE

Jillian Bolanz

SYNCING CYCLES: MOON, BODY, SOUL

It was a little after 7:00 pm on a frigid, early January evening in 2018. I was returning home from the chiropractor, and although my back felt better, I could still feel the pain of the bloat in my belly and the tears in the back of my throat. I knew at that point our little boys would be in bed, so I went in search of my husband, Michael, grateful to know I'd have the space for my big feelings to finally pour out.

I found Michael in my hybrid home-office-gym. He was ready to exercise, pulling up a streaming workout on the computer. He looked up at me and smiled, but quickly replaced that with a look of concern upon seeing my weary expression.

I took a breath and spoke words I hadn't realized until that moment had been bottled up for years: "I feel broken." As soon as I said them, I felt something shift within me; it was like a truth that I'd tried to shove down and ignore was finally coming to the surface. I couldn't ignore it anymore.

. . .

"I'm a healthy, young woman who takes care of herself," I said as I moved a set of dumbbells and sat on the workout bench. "I can clearly have babies, so WHY?! Why don't I get a period? Why am I so bloated and blocked all the time? Why don't I have a full cycle?" The tears poured down as I finally asked the question out loud that my body had been asking for years: *why?*

At 32 years old, I hadn't had a natural period in fourteen years. When I was 18, after a handful of teenage years having very irregular and harsh periods, I went on birth control. I got a monthly period between the ages of 18-25, but I knew they came because of the hormones packed into that little blue package of pills. When my husband and I decided it was time to start trying for babies, I was so excited and ready to get off birth control. My period never returned.

After years of trying, I had my first baby in 2013 and my second in 2016. Both sweet boys were conceived by way of the IUI process (the stage right before IVF) and I remember the doctor looking at me and saying, "We can either figure out why you don't have a period, or we could just get you pregnant." At that time of my life, when I heard his words I was equal parts relieved and ecstatic! The truth was, back then I didn't care why I didn't have a period; in fact, I felt like I'd beat the system somehow: *you mean I don't HAVE to get a period, slow down, feel weak and emotional and I can still have babies?*! Leading up to this conversation, I preferred to do all things quickly, efficiently, and at a level that would exceed everyone's expectations. Force and overdrive were my go-tos, so not getting a period, with all its emotions and need to slow, seemed super convenient for many years. I quickly responded to the doctor, "Just get me pregnant!" By the grace of God/Goddess/Universe and modern day medicine, we did!

. . .

But five years, two magickal babies, and one dark night with a body that was perpetually in pain later, I wanted to know the answers to the first question that doctor asked me: *why?*

This question was the true beginning of my spiritual awakening. It's what brought me to the moon and her cycles. It's what taught me about energy and how my body was doing exactly what I was trying to do in life: holding on tight, never slowing down, trying to force, grip, and control. There had to be a better way and that night I made a commitment to step through the sacred portal that was created the moment I asked *why*. I was ready to know, love, and trust myself.

The next morning, after that sacred conversation with Michael and the moment of honesty with myself, it was time to get to work. I knew there were appointments to book and research to do, but oddly, I didn't feel overwhelmed by these logistical tasks. I felt centered. For the first time ever, I'd be supporting my external work with deep, self-discovery, inner work. It was like something in me sighed a breath of relief. I was ready to ask questions and seek answers in a new way. I was ready to ask not just doctors, specialists, and experts, "*Why?*", but also myself.

The team I built was amazing. I started working with pelvic floor physical therapists, naturopaths, and acupuncture specialists. I brought my coach, my chiropractor, and my family up to speed about my desire and willingness to reconnect with my female cycle. I felt deeply supported by all of them, and most importantly, I felt incredibly supported by myself. I trusted the professionals would provide me with many answers, but I also knew that there would be some answers that only I'd be able to uncover. So, a journal, pen, and plethora of introspective focused books were enlisted as I added myself to the roster.

March 2018 arrived. I was driving along a road that boarded a marsh, headed toward the ocean on an unseasonably warm early spring day. It was the perfect setting to ensure my one-year-old would nap as I drove. I breathed in the sweet air and listened to one of the many audio books I'd purchased since that January night. Entitled *The Woman Code* by Alisa Vitti, It was a pretty clinical book with lots of science that my brain found super interesting. My heart, however, carried an unexplained yearning for more. I was suddenly aware of a deep knowing within myself, a place of wisdom, that had awakened that night in my office. The information I'd gathered, appointments I'd been to, and numerous lab tests were mostly fascinating and helpful. However, I continued to hear a whisper from my heart: "Keep digging, there is so much more to be discovered."

I continued along my marshy route and smiled at the brave and bundled up, early season kayaker. The ocean would be in view momentarily and as I sat up taller for the first glimpse of the glittery watertop, I heard it – the line that my heart had been waiting for! "The moon cycle is 28 days and so is our female cycle." It was such a simple statement, but I felt my entire body light up with both celebration and relief. It felt like a beautiful activation of learning something new and remembering something that had been there, on a primal level, all along. I'd learned enough, at this point in my sacred motherhood journey, to know that my son was sleeping deeply enough for me to turn the volume up. And I did.

The small section about the connection between our female cycle and the moon cycle didn't give me too much specific information, but enough to invite me into knowing that *this* was the place I was headed with my inner work. The author invited me to realize that the fact that the moon cycle and the female cycle were the same length wasn't a coincidence. She presented that the moon was constantly ebbing and flowing and no two days of her cycle were exactly alike; so why did we, as women, think we needed to act the same each day? I couldn't wait to get home to my journal and find connections between the phases of the female cycle and the moon cycle.

With the ocean on my left, whose very tides are governed by the pull of the moon, I knew I'd found it. I would take the tinctures from my naturopath and do the exercises my physical therapist suggested, but it was up to me to go on a journey to explore the magical luminary in the sky. A portal had opened and I was going in!

My audible list was suddenly filled with fewer books on the physical body and as many books I could find about the moon. My focus had gone from the ailments of my physicality to the energy that flowed through her. So much was coming up, really quickly. For most of my life, I'd been defining my worth by my output. Because of this, I felt the need to always be hustling, grinding, and forcing. Whether that was forcing myself to stay up an extra hour to do more work or forcing myself to put on a happy face, I was always set to "on" (waxing, in moon terminology). In fact, the only times I'd let myself truly rest (wane) were when I'd pushed myself past the point of burnout and would be forced - there's that word again - to stop. This, of course, only resulted in feeling guilty and worthless because I couldn't do anything. So, as soon as I was able, I'd be back to the races again, feeling like I needed to make up for lost time.

I truly believe that this way of forceful living is what took a toll on my personal cycle. I was always waxing and never waning. I was always going and never resting. I was gripping through my actions which resulted in a clenching in my body. There was no flow to my approach to life, and as such, there was no menstrual flow. The feminine cycle is creation and lifeforce; and, in focusing only on the "doing," I was depriving myself of the "being" half of a healthy, rhythmic cycle. I was not fully participating with my own life force!

During the early days of my moon discovery journey, I focused a lot on the concept of waxing and waning. To keep it super simple, I broke the moon cycle into two sections: the waxing cycle is from New Moon to Full Moon and the waning cycle is Full Moon back to New Moon. This was powerful for me. With this simple shift in perspective, I started becoming conscious of my emotions after a long time of disconnection.

I remember being a deeply feeling child with big emotions and a big heart. As I grew, those emotions were always there, but much like menstruating, I feared that feeling the depths of my emotions would slow me down and that wasn't a thing I was ready to do. I got good at shoving anything I didn't want to feel to the side and pressing on with whatever task my to-do list had for me. When I started working with the moon, however, I could feel a resurfacing and reconnection to my emotions and I welcomed it!

The moon herself is said to be deeply intertwined with our emotional self. The moon doesn't generate her own light but rather reflects the sun's light back to us. In so doing, she invites us to go deeper into ourselves, to feel our way through our experiences, look at the shadows, and dance in the illumination. When I began working with the moon, not only was I feeling more deeply, but I was witnessing the plethora and range of emotions that came up for me. More importantly, still, I witnessed how my emotions, like the moon herself, would wax and wane over time.

. . .

It was through witnessing my emotions and the ways they showed up that I felt encouraged to dive deeper into the moon's phases. I began learning and living the eight phases of the moon cycle the same way I'd experienced every part of this journey so far: with deep gratitude and awe. I couldn't believe that living in this connective, cyclical, natural way had taken me 32 years to discover; but now that I had discovered it, there was no going back!

I grieved for the former version of me who truly believed she needed to hustle and grind every day of her life. I was so sad that I went for so long believing that my worthiness was based on my productivity and output. I felt so badly for all those times I had forced myself to continue when, on a primal level, I begged for a reprieve. But above all else, I felt so grateful to know that I'd never have to return to that way of living and I had Mumma Moon to guide the way.

Breaking the moon cycle into eight phases felt so natural to me as soon as I learned about the essence of each phase. For every waxing phase, there is a waning phase that immediately follows it. To me, this was incredibly important to understand. The natural essence of cyclicality is to go and then be. Not even the moon remains in waxing energy for more than 3.5 days in a row before she steps into a waning phase! If even she needed to wane every other phase, what made me think I was an exception to this cyclical rule?

During one early summer's evening, several months into my work with the moon, I sat in front of the fire with my journal and calendar. I wrote about each of the moon phases and doodled where the phases connected into a typical female cycle. I marked on my calendar where each phase would end and another would begin. I made a commitment to myself that night, to get to know myself deeper than I ever had before. I promised to make note, daily, of how I felt each day and which phase the moon was in the sky. I knew, over time, this would give me incredible insight as I'd start to see patterns of how I felt during different phases. Not only would this let me honor my feelings exactly where they were, but I'd be able to better support myself through future moon cycles.

I found it amazing how allowing myself to flow with the moon simultaneously enhanced my experience with my own cyclical flow. From letting my emotions flow through a full range of feelings to tapping into the flowy essence of a menstrual cycle, I was in awe of the available synchronicity. I drew so much wisdom and light from the moon cycle itself and honored the ever-changing needs of my physical and emotional bodies as a result. This was truly life-changing work.

By connecting with the moon phases, not only was I discovering how incredible my capacity to feel was but I began trusting myself to honor and tend to myself with a loving compassion I'd never done before. This developing trust allowed me to not only meet my needs, but it began to inform my great work in the world as an Intuitive Coach. I started teaching about the moon phases to other women, to remind them of their primal, cyclical nature, so that they could stop forcing, and start flowing through life in their sacred way. I created sacred spaces, in person and virtually, where women could come and emote, share, and feel safe practicing this new way of living.

I tracked my feelings and the cycles for months. I fell in love with the moon, with flow, and myself! I worked with my team of providers, listened to my intuition, excitedly shared about all I was learning. It was a fun summer filled with discovery and sacred breakthroughs, that all led to one divinely mind-blowing day: August 8, 2018. On this day, for the first time naturally, in over 14 years, I bled. I felt simultaneously shocked and yet, unsurprised; I was elated and grateful, but there was also a feeling of calm. I heard an inner whisper: "of course, you got your period," which flooded through me. Because of the work I'd done, the flow I'd committed to, and the connection I'd forged between Mumma Moon and my true self, I experienced a full female cycle. And I truly thought that was the end of the miracle.

My period came a handful of times over the course of the next Wheel of the Year. My cycle never synced to the 28 days of the moon cycle, but the time between periods got closer and closer with each bleed until July of 2019. I woke up and realized my period was taking longer this cycle than the one previous. With that, a thought struck me. It was a thought I had never considered before; I'd been told it couldn't happen without medical support. The two babies I'd had via that medically supported route affirmed that notion. However, a lot had changed in a year and that thought prompted me to take a pregnancy test. Getting my period, it turned out, was not the end of the miraculous journey. I was pregnant!

Working with the moon cycle changed my life completely. I felt more attuned to my emotions, my divine flow, and my body. And on February 22, 2020, I welcomed our third miraculous son into the world.

We all have our sacred paths, divine timing, and personal nuances to our human experience. We all have a personal connection to the moon that cannot be duplicated because of our individual uniqueness. However, her energy is universally available to us all and when we learn to sync to it in our own sacred ways, the miracles that are available for us abound! I'll never forget how broken I felt that January 2018 night. I'll forever be grateful for the space Michael held for me as I asked, "*why*", and to myself for being open to learning in more ways than I could have ever imagined. May we wax and wane, go and be, and honor our truth, with Mumma Moon lighting our way, forevermore.

Moon Phases & Energy Descriptions

An entire moon cycle is +/- 28 days depending on different astrological occurrences. For the sake of easy math, we will work with a 28 day moon cycle and connect into eight phases that last 3.5 days each. It's also important to say that these phases and our energetic, physical, and emotional connection to them are fluid. There are no hard starts and stops with the moon phases. The energy of one flows into the energy of the next. We each have our own personal connection to the phases and at times, can feel the energy of a coming phase earlier or later than it officially arrives. Understanding the energy that is universally available to us with the eight moon phases is incredible. Developing our own personal relationship to this universal energy though? It's life changing!

New Moon

The first phase of the moon cycle is the New Moon. The New Moon is when the moon is in the same location in the sky as the sun, and as such can't be seen as it is consumed by the sun's rays and thus can't reflect light back to us here on Earth. At night, the sky appears dark and moonless. This is a time to begin again or embark on something new. The New Moon is a waxing phase and is a time to set intentions for that moon cycle. Two powerful questions I love to ask myself during the New Moon phase are: "What do I want to *do* over the next cycle?" and "How do I want to *feel* over the next cycle?" These questions allow me to honor my waxing energy with the "do" question and waning energy with the "feel" question. Setting intentions with the New Moon allows you to purposefully pave the way for what you'd like to focus on. This results in you more consciously participating in life by co-creating with energy that is universally available to you.

Crescent Moon

The second phase of the moon cycle is the Crescent Moon. This is the first waning phase of the cycle where we let the intentions we actively set during the New Moon to really integrate into our bodies. Humans often try to skip this step; we are taught to set a goal and then go after it. The Crescent Moon reminds us that we need to believe in things before we see them. Cultivating that belief for what we'd like to manifest in our mind and feeling it in our bodies will help us to know that it is done before we even start working for it.

First Quarter Moon

The third phase of the moon cycle is the First Quarter Moon phase. In this phase, it's time to get to work! In the waxing First Quarter Moon phase we are finally able to take action on our intentions, now that we've set them and allowed for them to integrate into our being. It is of ultimate importance to harness your energy and take actionable steps with discernment during this phase. We want to have a plan and do first things first and second things second so we can channel our boundless energy. It's easy during the First Quarter Moon to want to do all the things; however, that usually results in scattered, half-completed projects. Instead, we are going for impact-ful, intentional action that will move the needle forward with this phase.

Gibbous Moon

The fourth phase of the moon, and final phase of the first half of the cycle, is the Gibbous Moon. This phase is a waning phase and it's a perfect time to put on your best investigator hat and collect some data. At the gibbous moon, we have the opportunity to reflect on all that's happened so far. Questions like, "What's working?", "What's not working?", "How am I feeling?", and "Do my intentions still apply or do I need to make changes?" are great ways to get really present with your current state, where you've been, and where you'd like to go. There is no need to do anything right now. Emotionally we get to tend to ourselves after taking big, potentially vulnerable, action. Energetically we get to witness where we've been and what we will celebrate and release at the next moon phase.

Full Moon

In the light of the Full Moon, everything is illuminated! Those things (habits, patterns, beliefs, stories, etc.) that often find dark corners within us to hide with are lit up, for there are no shadows when the moon is the biggest and brightest in the sky! At the Full Moon, we celebrate and release. We celebrate what's working and release what's not; sometimes we even celebrate what we release because it creates space to bring in something new! It's super important to leave judgment out of the practice of releasing; sometimes with this waxing energy, we want to leverage what isn't working as a tactic to shame ourselves. When we can remember that everything is working out in our favor and to celebrate where we've been and what we know now, we can move forward with so much more ease, fun, and a well-lit path.

Disseminating Moon

The sixth phase of the moon is a waning one and calls us into deeply nourishing and nurturing ourselves. We danced, celebrated, and released under the Full Moon; and now, it's time to go inward. The Disseminating Moon is a time when energetically we can feel a little tender by all the output we just participated in. During this phase, going slow, soothing ourselves, asking ourselves how we can best love and support ourselves, and then actually doing that is so powerful.

. . .

Third Quarter Moon

The Third Quarter Moon is the time of ultimate reward! This very action-oriented, waxing phase is where we get to do all the things and we have the energy to support ourselves because we took exquisite care of ourselves in the Disseminating Moon phase. During the third quarter moon, we get to reap what we've sown. The intentions we set back at the New Moon are resulting in manifestations! Also, because of the space we made by releasing what no longer serves us at the Full Moon, we can plant new seeds for the future. It's a time to receive the benefits of the inner and outer work we've put in while riding that creation energy and setting ourselves up for success again!

Balsamic Moon

The final phase of the Moon Cycle is the Balsamic phase; it's the deep, appreciative sigh at the end of a meaningful cycle's work. The Balsamic Moon is a waning moon and the energy is that of quiet appreciation. It's a time for reflection. During this phase we look back at all we have done and how we've felt. We get to generate a feeling of pride in our commitment to our intentions and willingness to pivot along the way to best support ourselves, all cycle long. During this phase, we know that another cycle approaches. There will be another New Moon and another chance to set intentions again. But not yet. We get to be right where our feet are knowing that this moment matters. Reflecting back with gratitude matters. Resting and appreciating matters so that when the time comes, we'll be ready to create again. And for now, we can simply be.

About the Author

JILLIAN BOLANZ

Jillian Bolanz is an Intuitive Life Coach, Spiritual Mentor, and Reiki Master of Masters. She is a guidess of all things moon, cyclicality, intuition, and True-Self love. The creator of the deeply connective and soul-embodying coaching programs, the True You School and the True You Tent, Jillian's mission is to help women to stop forcing and start flowing in life so that they can uncover the truth of who they really are. Jillian creates safe, sacred containers to help women honor their connection to spirituality and their personal power. Leveraging the power of the moon, seasons, and all things cyclicality, she supports her soulmate clients as they reconnect to their intuition, their divine cycle, and their inner magick by way of energetically immersive coaching and sisterhood experiences.

Jillian has been featured on Maine's NBC news station and multiple podcasts and coaching platforms. When she's not coaching her beloved clients, leading moon circles, or facilitating her True You Live events, you'll find Jillian out for a run in the Maine sunshine or hanging with her husband, Michael, and their sons, Cameron, Andrew, and Nathan.

Find Jillian here:

LinkTree: https://linktr.ee/jillianbolanz

IG: @jillianbolanz

TikTok: @jillianbolanz

FB: https://www.facebook.com/jillian.leger.bolanz

facebook.com/jillian.leger.bolanz

instagram.com/jillianbolanz

TWO

Marsha Stultz

THE LIBERATION AND HEALING OF THE WOUNDED INNER CHILD

A return to authenticity and self-love

How do any of us get to be who we are? We are a collection of all our life experiences, our failings and successes, our wounds, and our healing. I have had a private practice in energy healing therapy for over thirty years and in that time, I have seen some common threads surface in the healing journey of most of my clients. I see these as golden nuggets for our evolution as we heal through them. I want to share one such golden nugget with you; healing the wounded inner child.

We all have inner child aspects. Who we are today is not just the age we are now, but rather an amalgam of every age we have ever been and every experience we've ever had. I feel my healthy inner child active when I'm spontaneous, creative, and curious. However, I've had wounded aspects of my inner child who have held my pain, insecurities, and suffering before healing them. This interfered with my enjoyment of life. These wounded parts made me uncomfortable in groups of people. I felt insecure and unworthy. My wounded inner child would tell me things like, "My opinion doesn't matter" or "What I could contribute wasn't worthwhile", and "Everyone knows more than me and has better ideas." I was constantly giving my power away to people. That got old!

How does the inner child get wounded? When we're young, we are deeply impacted by those who raise us and have power over us. For most of us, that's our family, caregivers, and educators. They can both positively and negatively impact us. In my experience, there are many ways the wounding can happen. Let's look at three major ways this can happen.

The first way can happen while we're in the womb of our mother. When we are developing in the uterus for about 9 months we are also sitting in our mother's sacral chakra. I want to take a moment here in case you are not familiar with the chakras and give you a brief understanding of what they are, and the important role they play in our health and overall well-being.

Here is a brief summary of some of the attributes of the 7 major chakras to help you understand why this is so impactful to us as children and our development into adulthood:

The root chakra is located between the legs coming down from the tailbone, and relates to our basic needs for survival: food, clothing, and shelter; It also signals to us certain choice points when we're threatened: fight, flight, or freeze. There can be a lot of fear there.

. . .

The sacral chakra is located between the naval and the pubic bone. This is where we hold our deepest emotions, our trauma, issues related to sex and sexuality, creativity, flow, money, and nurturing.

The will center chakra is located between the naval and V in the ribs or solar plexus area, and it is about our ability to trust our truth, take action, and move forward in the world.

The heart chakra is located at the center of the chest, (some people have a two-heart chakra system). It's how we experience love, both giving and receiving love. Love of our tribe, family, community, and the world all happen here.

The throat chakra, located at the throat, is how we express the energy of the other chakras: talking, screaming, singing, whispering, or choosing to say nothing.

The third eye chakra, located above the brow line in the center of the forehead, is about our inner vision, our intuition and is balanced with our intelligence.

The crown chakra, located at the crown of the head, is about our deep connection with source energy.

Now that we have a common understanding of the chakras, let's go back to the sacral chakra and think about how we marinate there for nine months in our mother's womb in all our mother's healed and unhealed issues relating to those topics. And as a fetus, we can take on those energies as if they were our own. We can carry those emotions and wounds of not only our mother, but our grandmother and back through the ancestral lineage as if they were our own issues and emotions. Female fetuses have all their eggs fully formed before birth and may absorb and hold trauma from the ancestral lineage ready to pass on to the next generation. This means before we're even born, we can absorb unresolved trauma from our mother and even our ancestors; and if we don't resolve it, we can potentially pass it down to the next generation! This can be the first major wounding to the inner child before she's even born.

The second major way wounding can happen is through the impact of people's words.

We all know words can hurt but children are especially vulnerable. As a child develops, the brain goes through stages of brain wave activity over time that impact how a child experiences and processes events within their environment. Adults, the majority of the time, are in beta brain wave activity. This is what we would call our normal waking state. However, from the time we are a fetus until 2 years of age, our brainwave activity is in delta. Delta is a very slow, deep hypnotic state where we are highly suggestible. It is the brain-wave state of deep sleep or very deep meditation. This means that the words we hear and the energy we feel goes into our subconscious as the Truth! When we get negative messages such as "Why do you cry all the time," "Stop talking," "I wish you were never born," "What's wrong with you," "Why did I have another child!" or worse, these messages can become part of our belief system about ourselves even though we were pre-verbal when we heard it.

From ages 2-6 years old, the brain wave activity is mostly in theta. Not quite as deep as delta, but still a deep meditative state where we are very susceptible to suggestion and are subconsciously programmed by our experiences.

· · ·

30

From 6-12 years of age, we are mostly in alpha brain wave activity, the beginning phase of sleep, and the beginning phase of meditation. It is the state where the words and actions of others are still strong suggestions that influence our concepts of self.

The third major way we can be wounded as children is through the chakras and auric fields of our family and caretakers. We've briefly described the chakras; here's a description of the aura. The aura is a field of vibrating energy particles that create a field of energy around our physical body that reflects our core beliefs and thoughts. It is a part of our protection, and part of how we sense and perceive our environment.

Our chakras and auric fields don't fully develop until we are about 7 years old. This is important because we are enveloped in our caregiver's chakra and auric systems that greatly influence the natural development of our chakras and auric fields. Just like we tend to parrot our parent's opinions until we learn about the world and develop our own opinions, the same is true of our chakras and aura. As our chakras develop, they can mimic that of our primary caregivers. For example, if our parents are very fear-based or untrusting, not only will we think those ways, but our energy systems will also reflect those same patterns which can impact our choices, making us more fearful and untrusting not just as children but throughout our adult lives. Our chakras not only impact us energetically but also physically because they are energetically connected to, or reflex to, our endocrine glands and hormonal secretions which influence our moods, thoughts, and relationships. Literally every part of our lives is impacted by the health of our chakras.

The auric field of our caregivers can impact us as well. We can develop the same patterns as our mother or primary caregiver which, if not healthy, can limit us. An example of this would be feeling too vulnerable in the world or unwilling to let people in emotionally.

I could write volumes about the chakras and auric fields, but this tiny bit of information will give you the idea. When people are living a life they love, or they understand their energy systems and support them to function optimally, their chakras and aura are beautiful and support them to live the life they want. However, people who are not aware of their energy systems and are living a life they don't want and feel stuck can have very compromised, or barely functioning chakras. These people generally feel unhappy, discouraged, and disempowered. We all are, on a subconscious level, programmed by our mother and father, family members, or care-givers from the time of conception until we begin to question what we believe and ask ourselves why we believe it.

This did not just happen in our generation. It has been happening forever, generation after generation. Everyone is operating from some deep wounds until they are on their own healing journey. For me, this explains why the world is the way it is. Remember, this is about the liberation and healing of the wounding that can happen in childhood and affect us later as adults.

I want to share some of my story to help pull this all together for you. I was born to a working-class family in a small town in Maine. My dad was in the army in World War ll. He was in two battles, Normandy and the Battle of the Bulge. Most American soldiers did not survive but my dad did. When the war was over, he came back to Maine to his small hometown on the Kennebec River and married his high school sweetheart. He got a job as an apprentice plumber and learned a trade. A year and a half later they had their first child, a son, three years later a second child, a daughter, and built a small home across the river. Eight years after that I was born.

By then things in our family were starting to unravel. My early memories were of some family fun and a lot of fighting. My father drank a lot. My mother was clinically depressed. My mom worked and my dad always had two jobs.

He worked at Brunswick Naval Air Station as a civilian plumber by day, and evenings and Saturdays worked for himself on small plumbing jobs around town. My mom often worked some evenings and Saturdays as a clerk in retail. She was exhausted, emotionally needy, and depressed. She couldn't really parent me. So, I parented her. She couldn't talk about any subject that was hard or uncomfortable. My siblings were very loving, fun, and sweet to me. However, I was only 8 when my brother moved out of the house and I was 12 when my sister moved out. Then, I was on my own.

I remember Sundays growing up and how painful they were. It would start Saturday night which typically was the biggest drinking night for my dad. My father would act resentful toward my mother, complaining to her "Why can't you just have a little fun once in a while?" She would say "There's nothing fun about watching you make a damn fool of yourself." By Sunday morning my parents would not be speaking to each other. My dad would go down to the basement and tinker in his workshop alone and sulk. Mom would be depressed and play the role of the victim, changing all the beds, doing mountains of laundry, and even though everybody dreaded it, she would make a big Sunday dinner. By the time dinner was served, the tension in the air was so thick you could cut it with a carving knife. Dad would criticize the meal, "Over-cooked" he'd say and the fighting would start again, usually ending with my mother leaving the dinner table in tears. My father would act dejected, and they would both go to separate rooms to nap. My sister and I would have to clean up the kitchen in the sullen house we both just wanted to escape from. Then, after my sister moved out it was me with them at the dinner table doing the dishes alone wanting to escape. I felt like it was my job to make both my parents feel loved and make everything better. A big job for a kid.

The older I got the worse family life became. When I started to mature and have boyfriends my father seemed to reject me. Nobody ever really talked about the tension and stress in our family. My father would get drunk every night. At first, he would be sweet, and several drinks in turn mean. Every time I walked into the room or came home I had to assess the emotional climate to decide how to act and what to do, I felt as if big dark clouds continuously hung in the sky above our home. The older I got, the worse our relationship got. By my last year of high school, he rarely even spoke to me. My mother was not coping well. She was barely functioning, she would go to work as an ed. tech at a middle school, come home, change into a bathrobe, pull the shades, and do nothing but chain smoke and cry sitting on the couch in the dark. I rebelled. I was rarely home except to sleep. I hated being in that house. In my twenties as a young adult, I acted out the patterns I picked up from my family and attracted partners who couldn't really love me, who were depressed and wounded. I felt unlovable to the core. And I was angry!

Two days after my 29th birthday my dad died. I felt great sadness, but I also felt relief. Then I started feeling angry. I was in therapy at the time with a wonderful therapist who helped me understand that I was beginning to have memories of early childhood sexual abuse. I had completely suppressed these events but now that my father was dead it was safe for me to begin to realize the depth of dysfunction in my family. This was around the same time I was finishing up college with a double major in social work and women's studies. I also started to study various forms of energy work and began developing my psychic abilities. I had an amazing circle of women friends who stood by me through my healing process and with the support of great healers, my therapist, and friends, I embarked on an amazing healing journey.

I remember a vision I had around this time while taking a bubble bath one evening. Feeling relaxed, I began to wonder how my father got to be who he was. I had a vision of him as a small child saying, "Why don't you care about me?" with big tears in his eyes. It startled me and broke my heart. I started wondering what happened to him in his life that turned him into the father I knew. I wanted to be angry at him and blame him for everything that went wrong in my life but this vision made that harder to do. The more I worked on healing myself, I began to explore my father's past. I realized my dad didn't consciously choose to sexually abuse me, or be an alcoholic, or be unable to talk about his feelings. His primary emotion was anger. Looking back, I think he was in a lot of emotional pain and running on unconscious programming from his childhood and the war. Sadly, he developed throat cancer and completely lost his ability to speak. He died at 64.

I learned from his younger brother that Dad came home from the war a different man. There were no services for PTSD; it wasn't even a diagnosis then. It was the attitude of "pull yourself up by your bootstraps and get on with life." The war changed him. I wanted to be mad at him, to blame him still. Other soldiers came home from war and didn't do what he did. I then began to wonder; what was his childhood like? What sort of a home did he grow up in?

My dad was the oldest of 4 children, two sisters after him and 13 years later a little brother. He was left-handed and slightly dyslexic. They were a Catholic family, so he went to a Catholic school where the nuns tied his left hand behind his back and forced him to become right-handed. The dyslexia and perhaps being forced to become right-handed gave him a learning disability so he didn't thrive academically, unlike his sister who was valedictorian of her class. All his siblings went to college except my father. His father, my grandfather, was an alcoholic and blatantly cheated on his wife. I remember a story my mother told me from her childhood. Her family and my father's family lived on the same maple tree-lined street and she was playmates with one of his sisters. One day as they were playing outside a very pregnant woman walked by and Dad's sister said to Mom, "That's my father's girlfriend." Like everyone already knew! He was of course married to my grandmother who was busy raising four children.

I grew up living next door to my grandfather. His wife, my grandmother, died when I was one. He died when I was ten. I have no conscious memory of being abused by my grandfather, my therapist had concerns about my recurring nightmares of being trapped in his attic and being chased by something, and never being able to get to the door, or if I did or it was blocked by something or someone. I would wake up in a panic with my heart pounding, feeling terrified..I felt like "Now, I have someone to blame". It's all my grandfather's fault! How could he? How dare he?"

But then, after some time, I thought what was my grandfather's life like? With a little digging, another painful story emerged. My grandfather was born in northern Maine, He had 3 brothers. I know he was near the younger end of the sibling group from a family photo I saw. I don't have a lot of information about his family, but I do have enough to put together a picture of some parts of his life. His name was Frank and when he was around 7 or 8 his father died. His family had no money to speak of and all the boys went to live on different farms as workers while their mother went to work as a housekeeper for an older man who had lost his wife. She worked there until she saved enough money to bring her family back together and I don't know how long that was. I assume it was at least a year, maybe longer. My poor grandfather, a small child all alone, found himself on a farm expected to work with no family to care for him. I do know his older brother was working and living at a nearby farm, and one Sunday a month the two brothers got to spend the afternoon together. That was it! I don't know what happened to him on the farm with no one to protect him. Life on a farm in northern Maine is a tough life for anyone, least of all a young child.

This broke my heart. This little boy, all alone in the world. How could I blame him? I was beginning to understand there is no one to blame! As I learned about brainwave states and the impact on child-hood development, the chakras, and time in the womb, I realized we are all walking around wounded on some level. And, equally, we are all doing the best we can. Every generation is impacted by the generations before until we wake up and consciously begin to heal.

I was inspired to continue to study, learn, and grow. I was no longer attracted to people who couldn't show up for me and ended up meeting the love of my life, who is and continues to be, loving and present. I built a great life for myself, committed to my own healing journey. I have had wonderful mentors, studied with brilliant heal-ers, quantum scientists, and visionaries around the world, and continue to learn, grow, and evolve. I became a self-loving person inspired to help others help themselves through my work. I built a private practice as a healer, working with amazing clients. I learned much from observing my clients' evolution in their work with me.

I have developed a deep and rich relationship with my Guides. They teach me about healing and show me new techniques that have been powerful healing tools for myself and my clients. They have helped me develop new cutting-edge work and have helped create my Heart Lotus Evolution certification program, Healing with

Sacred Geometry program, the Energy of Business program, and many others. There is a particularly powerful piece of work my Guides helped me create I want to share with you for healing the Wounded Inner Child. But first, let's talk about how we recognize those wounded inner child aspects within us.

Let me ask you a question: Have you ever experienced this; You are in a conversation with someone and you are present and feeling like an adult and all of a sudden they say something that triggers an old deep feeling that makes you feel angry, defensive, powerless, or shut down and most likely unsafe as well? Maybe you don't know why but there is no longer an adult behind the steering wheel of your life, just a child. We then typically react poorly or shut down. What's happening is your wounded inner child got triggered and is now behind the steering wheel of your life. The brain doesn't fully develop until age 25 so the inner child doesn't have the cognitive skills to reason, so she acts out, retreats, or both. It's hard to have a healthy relationship with someone's wounded inner child. In fact, it's not possible. Often in a vulnerable conversation, when one person's inner child gets triggered, the other person's inner child gets triggered as well. Who's minding the children?

Let's talk about why the wounded inner child is stuck and gets activated in the first place. When we have a trauma or scary experience as a child, we go into freeze mode. It is the response of the sympathetic nervous system. When we feel we're in danger we have a choice point for our nervous system: flight, fight, or freeze. Most often we freeze meaning the trauma does not get fully processed by our brain but is still there ready to be re-activated whenever we have an experience with a similar emotional vulnerability as the original trauma. This is the triggering of the wounded inner child. I say wounded child like we all only have one but most of us have enough to fill a baseball team.

. . .

I have developed a beautiful technique with the loving help and support of my Guides to help heal the wounded child aspects that is powerful and easy. The real healing comes from the child aspect getting the unconditional love and unconditional acceptance they needed in the first place; because the parent or caregiver was in their own wounded place at the moment of wounding you, they were unable to do so. It's likely they were in their own wounded inner child and acting out in their parenting or caretaking of you! Do you see the rabbit hole we're going down? Do you see how this can be an ancestral pattern that goes on for generations? Remember my story and what happened to me, my father, my grandfather?

Let the healing begin! This process is one of the ascension codes for living beyond your wildest dreams! When we break free from these patterns and heal, we are truly free. We can be authentic, creative, self-loving beings, stepping into our personal power, and become who we came here to be.

Think back to a time when your inner child was triggered. I invite you to not judge but rather be an observer. It's fascinating when we can detach and simply observe. Call on that sweet child, imagine she is there, comfort her as if she is there with you. Help her to feel safe, protected, loved. Call on The Divine- or God, Goddess, Buddha, Allah, Universe, whatever language works for you. I will call it Pure Source Energy. Call forth Pure Source Energy in the form of the Divine Mother and Divine Father. These are aspects of Pure Source Energy that have never been wounded, so all they know is unconditional love and unconditional acceptance. Let them scoop her up and love her without any wounding. They are re-parenting her. They might be holding her, or playing with her, telling her how amazing, special, and loved she is. Imagine the Divine Mother and Father validating her feelings, supporting her to be free and authentic, to see herself as lovable, safe, and empowered. Imagine her chakras beautifully open and aligned, her aura beautiful, clear, and radiant. Imagine all her energy systems in their Divine Radiant perfection. You don't need to know what that is- simply allow.

After you feel your little one is full of love and acceptance, happy and carefree, imagine her turning into the most beautiful light you can imagine and breathe that light in through your crown chakra and into the micro and macrocosm of your being, healed, whole and Holy.

When a child reaches the same age the parent was when they got wounded as a child, the parent can easily be triggered and have unreasonable expectations for their child. This is one-way parents begin to love conditionally. They have expectations of how and who their children should be. Through conditioning (conditional love and conditional acceptance) the parent breaks the spirit of the child to do what they need them to do to get love and approval. Sound familiar? This is not how anyone intends to parent but it is typical unconscious parenting unless the parent is awake and doing their own healing work.

You can do this process again and again with as many wounded child aspects as you can find. Be tender and loving with yourself in this process. You might want to take a detox bath. I recommend 1 cup baking soda and 1 cup sea salt added to a bath, maybe with some nurturing essential oils. This is very cleansing. Or, go for a walk, be in nature. Spend time talking to your inner children, asking them what they want. Let them have it. They might want to draw, learn an instrument, play, dance, eat ice cream. Indulge your inner little ones (yourself) in ways that are healthy, safe, and loving.

One of my teachers who is no longer on the Earth plane once channeled for a group of us the Egyptian God Toth. Toth was there to explain why we are born into our families of origin. He said that we choose our mothers carefully as they are our vessel to be in for nine months. He said being in the mother's womb with all her healed and unhealed traumas, ancestral traumas, and emotions she carries, gives our soul the opportunity to pick up or take on some of the issues. We do this to have the opportunity to heal on a soul level later and to help us remember our soul's mission for this incarnation! This helps us remember why we chose to come back and incarnate in this particular time-space continuum. He said offering to be a vessel to host the development of a soul coming into this world is a great service. Don't blame your mother, thank her. She, with all her wounds, was in service to your soul.

This means the wounding of the inner child and other difficult experiences we have are all opportunities to heal, wake up, and be on our true soul's journey. I invite us all not to be angry at our parents, but to have compassion and to hold for their healing. I invite you to love yourself well, heal and be happy. Who knows, your healing may well help your lineage. Many indigenous cultures believe that as we heal ourselves, the healing flows backward 7 generations and forwards 7 generations. This means that as we do our own healing to improve the quality of our lives, in the bigger picture we are also healing our soul wounds and releasing karma. Part of how we are releasing karma is healing the ancestral lineage and clearing the path of suffering for future generations, a noble cause indeed.

I see you, Healed Whole, and Holy. Blessed Be.

About the Author

MARSHA STULTZ

Marsha Stultz is a gifted healer, conscious channel, visionary, and teacher. She is an alchemist of energy healing. Her loving spirit and thirty plus years of experience create a safe, sacred, and nurturing environment to ignite your self-love and self-trust, so you can become who you came here to be. She is a midwife of ascension and Divine evolution seeing every moment as an opportunity to unconditionally love ourselves and each other. She offers private in-person and distance sessions, as well as many teachings, certifications, and gatherings. She has a BA in social work and women's studies, as well as certifications in many healing modalities.

Her great passion is certifying others in her beloved original modality, Heart Lotus Evolution. This is a profound evolutionary journey for healers, artists, parents, and anyone on the path of ascension.

She lives in Portland Maine with her amazing wife Mindy and three cats. In her spare time, she loves communing with nature, gardening, reading, singing, dancing, and socializing.

Find Marsha here:

Linktree: https://linktr.ee/marshastultz

THREE

Safrianna Lughna, MS

"THE QUEER-SPIRIT GUIDE"

Becoming the Butterfly

Beloved Being, I See You

Beautiful soul, I am so proud of you. You are moving forward, creating the reality you desire starting from within. Your heart is blossoming. Your soul is expanding. You are exactly where you need to be on this cosmic journey called life.

You are a part of something so important – far greater than any individual. Yet, it is your love for yourself on this journey that will ultimately help heal the planet.

Loving yourself isn't always easy though, is it?

You've survived hurt, confusion, and grief. You've experienced pain that eludes words and circumstances that left you wondering about the meaning of it all. You have survived moments when you thought it was all over. When you didn't know if you could go on. Moments where everything seemed hopeless. Meaningless. Times when it seemed you were living only for others, and not at all for yourself.

Butterfly Energy has brought me here. The medicine wisdom of this spiritual guide taught me that when we shift our perspective into one of witnessing, holding space, and loving ourselves, we can finally learn to fly. Then, we can rise above the societally made limitations and generational wounds with a higher perspective. Butterfly's lessons are but some of the codes for a New Earth timeline we are so in need of leaping onto as a Collective. But, to save the planet, we must first find and free ourselves from seemingly endless cycles of oppression, destruction, and apathy.

I offer to you glimpses of my story alongside Butterfly's medicine in the hopes that you, too, may see your journey as a natural part of this Earthly experience. It does not mean it is not without pain. Let me be clear: I do not stand for "toxic positivity" or simply washing away our sorrows. My wish is only for you to open to the possibility that maybe pain itself is not the enemy, but rather our judgment of it which ultimately leaves us feeling disconnected and dissatisfied with life.

Beloved being, I see you, and I believe in you.

The Caterpillar: Survival & Consumption

A caterpillar emerges from a glistening jewel-like egg, minuscule and fragile, yet ready to live. The butterfly will never exist if not for this early stage of consuming to survive.

· · ·

When we emerge from the womb, we immediately launch into a journey of consumption. Like the freshly hatched caterpillar, our mission is to eat and survive until the time comes when we're ready to build ourselves anew. That, however, takes time. Meanwhile, we are curious. Exploratory. Everything is magical. We want to taste, touch, smell, see, and hear it all because the experience of being in these sacred body vessels is exciting and fresh.

Unfortunately, many of us grew up feeding on trauma from multiple generations past, including our caregivers who so rarely knew the proper skills and tools needed to raise children. Instead of consuming peace, self-worth, and authenticity, many of us were left with scraps of drama, maladaptive coping, and often fierce individualism.

We live in a society that has externalized sources of power over and over again. So many look to teachers, doctors, politicians, and other authority figures for answers instead of looking within. This has been perpetuated from generation to generation, a legacy of pain and separation.

From our caterpillar stages, we are trained to comply with those in authority. Yet, the sense of dissonance we feel in distancing from our soul alignment leads to mental and physical health problems on a massive scale. It is no wonder that codependency is so prevalent in our culture. We are taught to defer to those we perceive as having power.

It is rare to meet someone who never experienced the "Because I said so," or " I'm the adult" schtick when they asked questions as a child. When we repeatedly hear dismissive statements like these, we can mistake the messages from our guardians and ancestors as facts.

Rather than exploring our sense of Self, we may feel shut down and adopt these outside messages as our "authentic identity."

My parents were not emotionally available when I was growing up, and my routines and structure were disrupted by fights, a divorce, and moving to a brand new state at nine years old. In this new life, I was forced into the role of a "parentified child," responsible for the emotions of the adults around me. This included being groomed and abused by a man four times my age. Rather than being fed autonomy and to identify my own values, dreams, and desires, my caregivers instead taught me how to manage others' feelings and ignore my own.

I sought comfort outside of myself, consuming everything I could without concern for how it might impact me. I threw myself into school as a distraction, staying up late to make each paper and project perfect so I could receive "healthy" approval. By 11, I'd already developed the habit of drinking whatever alcohol I could get my hands on to try and silence the voice inside me screaming that I was not okay. I binged on sugary snacks, trying to find the sweetness of life. I desperately tried to be comfortable – to find my exact place in this wild macrocosmic scheme of things. But, all my system knew was discomfort and pain.

Before I'd reached legal adulthood, I had already experienced the impact of neglect, domestic violence, divorce, sexual assault, abuse, poverty, and displacement. I was raised in a patriarchal society. I routinely dissociated and used self-harm to feel something other than detached, floating above my own body. By 15, I had survived three suicide attempts.

. . .

Like the caterpillar goes through the process of molting repeatedly in its early life, we too may find ourselves shedding the skins that no longer serve us. However, until we can recognize the energetic patterns that keep us feeling the same, we cannot fly. It took me what felt like ages to figure this out.

As a once-professional trauma therapist, I understand our biological system will naturally attempt to maintain the status quo, recreating energetic patterns we are familiar with to establish a sense of "safety." But, it's not *genuine* safety. It is our fried and frazzled, over-extended nervous system's attempt to ensure we don't encounter any of the terrifying unknown.

This meant even after the anguish and confusion of my childhood, I was not ready to transform. I was terrified. Although I recognized much of what had happened to me was not alright, I could not find myself. The only positive self-concept I could hold onto was that I was capable of anything – I'd survived horrors, after all. Yet, I found myself in more traumatic situations: toxic relationships mirroring my childhood experiences.

On my 18th birthday, I ran away from Maryland to Tennessee to be with a man I'd met in an online video game. He'd convinced me not to attempt suicide for the fourth time which to my young mind was the greatest kindness I'd ever been afforded. A few months later, we got married, resulting in a relationship that ended up loveless and disconnected. Over the course of our six-year marriage, we moved seven times, uprooting and displacing our life year after year. I leaned into sex work to make ends meet. As we faced the loss of our daughter in our final year together, I witnessed him emotionally withdraw for what seemed like the thousandth time. It was then I knew I needed to shed that skin. Still grieving, I left not for myself, but for another man.

. . .

After years of lovelessness (mirroring my relationship with my father), I leaped into a relationship with a narcissist. When he raped me on our third date and then told me he loved me, I felt frozen. When he held a gun to me and told me no one would care if I died, I accepted it. When he cheated on me for the third time, I thought it was fate. Despite recognizing right away that I was living out a domestic violence nightmare, I believed myself stuck. A majority of what I had consumed in my childhood was this same energy. In fact, this man reminded me so much of the one who used my underage body, it felt like a complete return to normalcy.

I installed the demeaning, cruel words of others into myself as beliefs, echoing the sentiments of people who could not even begin to see my worth because they could not see their own. I believed I was worthless aside from as a sexual object for men who had power over me. I believed it would never get better. My inherent worthiness and magic were tucked away, hidden beneath layers of a protective shell.

I didn't have an initial example of healthy reflection and emotional processing until I was in my mid-20s. After the loss of my child and first divorce, I put myself in therapy. My then therapist (now mentor) taught me the profound impact that holding a compassionate space for others could create. She demonstrated with grace what unconditional love felt like, even if I only got to experience it for an hour or two a week. Until then, I had just been taught to eat chocolate and ignore my feelings – shove them down deep and swallow them like a pill without water. I built shell after shell trying not to get hurt again, but it never worked.

. . .

It was during this time of self-development I knew, more than ever, that I wanted to be a healer and inspiration to others. I recognized how much of a difference it had made when someone simply showed up for me with presence and compassion. Once I'd seen that in another person, I, at last, consumed the information I needed to go into the darkness of my own self-healing.

In the past, I choked down any emotions that would cause other people discomfort. I'd witnessed repeatedly how attempts to use my voice were shut down. I stayed silent when I needed to speak my truth the most. I neglected my body and intuition. I abandoned my relationship with myself and the idea that I could preserve my sacred energy.

Now, I knew it was *possible* to experience unconditional love for myself simply because someone had offered it as an option. While one healthy example could not undo over two decades of non-stop trauma, I at least knew I could face my history and heal myself.

I'd survived, but survival was no longer enough.

The Chrysalis: Into the Dark

Merely a transitional state, the chrysalis provides a container in which the caterpillar can transform. From within this hard casing, she finds herself swimming in her own suffering, the soupy swelter of her undoing. She will unmake and remake herself in a grand new image.

Redesigning ourselves through the process of metamorphosis is far from glamorous. Who *really* wants to go into the sticky, sweltering goo of their darkest places – the spaces we feel overwhelmed, depressed, anxious, afraid, and disappointed?

How are we supposed to seek the light when we have only known the dark? I didn't know the answers, but I knew what I must do.

I knew I had to face the darkness fully, grieving the little caterpillar girl who had hurt so much. To fly, I saw I must be willing to delve down into the darkness of my greatest despair.

I placed my wedding ring down on the cluttered bedside table. Looking into the dark, wounded eyes of my second husband, I felt a profound shift in my body. I could see it in his, too. He knew I was done. I needed to find my true self beneath the layers of codependency I'd packed on like a suit of armor over the years.

Days before, I was standing in the rather bougie bathroom of a church washing my hands when I looked up and met my own eyes. Standing alone before the full wall mirror, I connected with myself in an entirely new way. Where before I had berated myself with judgment and diminished my worth, I suddenly experienced a jolt of life-altering self-love.

For years, I was stuck in a cycle of codependency and self-neglect. I couldn't do it anymore. I knew if I did, it would be my caterpillar death – this relationship would become the parasitoid wasp stinger finally piercing my heart. I had two choices: allow the last spark of hope in me to die, or leave my second marriage and accept it was not the "do-over" of my energetic past I longed for.

. . .

I recognized I was reenacting childhood wounds in my adult relationships, a piece of self-ownership that left me deeply depressed, depleted, and yet, somehow hopeful.

What unfolded in the coming year was messy. I left a long-term relationship, along with the business and home we tried to create together. Instead, I built my chrysalis. I put the boundaries up around myself I had struggled so much to uphold in the past, zipped myself up, and went into the unknown with only one wish: to find myself.

Initially, I was completely obscured. I could not access my inner wisdom and soul because all I could see was the misery of my first thirty years. I was drowning in my own gunk, traumatic residue, and negative self-beliefs that fully filled my crystalline cage.

During the first few months out of the relationship, I battled once again with suicidal thoughts. I wept daily. I was dissociated and disconnected from my support systems. My body felt like it was eating itself from the inside out. Whether it developed then, or I was just finally noticing it, I realized how much physical pain my body was in and soon received a diagnosis of fibromyalgia.

Even so, there was a deep inner knowing within me that if I could sit long enough in this soupy sorrow, something would shift. I recognized that if I could be gentle and learn to make myself anew even while experiencing the absolute agony of looking back on my past, then I could finally fly. Only then could I make myself in the image of beauty I was born to embody.

. . .

This dream kept me going. As I found scraps of grace for myself, I added them to my internal self-concept. I experimented from within the confines of my chrysalis to see what was authentic to me. I refused to be another woman ignored by the medical system and told to lose some weight. No matter what others told me I "should" do, I was going to keep hunting for the answers that were right for me and me alone.

I engaged in as many healing modalities as I could, prioritizing my limited finances to invest in myself. I used therapy, coaching, floating, meditation, acupuncture, massage, spiritual studies, and attending intensives and retreats to give myself the space to explore. I tried medication to help with the chronic depression I'd experienced and explored supplements, testing how each substance felt in my body. I started dancing around the living room in my pajamas again. I changed my diet to the ethically vegetarian one I wanted and felt most alive, rather than what others told me was right.

During this stage, I developed several meaningful relationships. Having finally transitioned from just consuming whatever was presented to me, I did my best to maintain health and boundaries every stage of the way. Nevertheless, I was not truly healed yet. I found myself giving all of my time to people who "needed" me, whether that was clients, romantic interests, friends, or my family. I overextended myself, all the while so *aware* of it. At times, it felt like I was watching myself from outside the cocoon, witnessing the unfolding of my new identity while actively unraveling the entirety of my past.

The shifting point was speaking up. My throat chakra, or energetic center of expression, had been shut down for years aside from my educational or professional roles. I began announcing to others when I was having difficulty breaking free from codependent patterns and sought out resources to help me reflect on my relationship with myself. I made a decision to live my life for myself, and to follow my own energy, values, and desires above all else; even if it meant leaving behind the shaky sense of safety I received when trying to "fit in" and manage others' expectations. And while I may have lost a few people along the way, I found myself.

The Butterfly: Flying Free

The butterfly frees herself from her chrysalis, the chamber where she has recreated herself from her own self-digestion. As she emerges, her wings with their shimmering scales will take time to strengthen so at last she can fly free.

Is there anything more beautiful than a butterfly in flight, delicate glittering wings still strong enough to lift her whole body through the sky? She has undergone true alchemy, changing her form and freeing herself to express her desires fully.

I recall the feeling of laying in the float tank completely submerged in darkness, silky water on my skin. Weightless and completely at ease, it was impossible to feel where I ended and the rest of my existence began. Peace radiated from my heart as I drifted in and out of consciousness and bliss.

While I don't experience bright images and movies playing out behind my eyes, I get little flickers and flutters of silhouetted shapes. From within the sensory deprivation chamber, I could see the image of myself as a butterfly emerging from her cocoon, her wings still damp and flimsy. I heard Spirit say to me, "You are the butterfly. Be patient with yourself, and soon you will soar."

· · ·

I knew then that I was finally emerging. I was transitioning from a place of *"Healing"* to one of *"Healed & Healing."*

This is a concept I describe often to my clients, those I serve as a guide, healer, and coach. Healing is something we will experience throughout our lives. We all come from the darkness into light when we are born. Then, at some point in our development (often repeatedly), we return to the darkness once again to experience a rebirth.

Through being able to experience the keen contrast between my past and present, I know I am only spiraling upward and moving towards more and more joy of being alive. I believe I had to experience the worst acts of lack of love to fully understand the power and potency of love. I chose to empower myself rather than to believe myself a victim of circumstances, powerless to write my own story.

Healing has been one of the most challenging yet rewarding experiences of my life, and I truly appreciate myself, everything I've been through, and the power of contrast all the more. Without those experiences, I would not be able to be a voice for those who have been stepped on, taken advantage of, or otherwise abused. I would have no idea, truly, what it is like to walk a mile in their shoes, to understand how difficult it can feel to heal. Now I know exactly what I want to attract to me and have the necessary boundaries, beliefs, and support systems needed to ensure I do not violate my own energy again.

Because of this journey, I understand being a healer is not actually about healing others. It is about teaching people the capacity they have to heal themselves. By existing as my fullest self, I offer an alternative to the status quo, trauma-lead, societally scripted lives so many feel forced to live. I encourage others to cross the bridge from a state of healing all the time into a state of being healed and healing.

When we've reached the *healed* stage, we have mastered the most important energy that exists: love. When we have healed, we love ourselves completely even though we are still healing. When we can love ourselves in the darkness, be kind to ourselves through any pain, and allow ourselves the fullness of our existence without giving into judgment, numbing, anger, or fear, we have achieved Heaven on Earth.

Healing is ongoing work. That's why we *must* take care of ourselves and put our energy first. There will always be obstacles here for our embodied forms that will get in the way of us experiencing lasting "happiness." However, it's possible to experience lasting love.

When you choose to experience healing, may it not be because you feel you have to heal everything *right now*, but rather because you understand the value and the importance of putting yourself first. May you experience the bliss of being healed, knowing you *are* love and loved even as you struggle. You are a beautiful butterfly at your core, no matter what stage you're at in life. And you *will* fly.

Butterfly Wisdom

Butterfly medicine offers you the following wisdom to call on whenever you need it:

• Be like the caterpillar and remember you are what you eat. Consume love through self-care of all kinds, from nourishing words of wisdom to the right company. Shed your skin when it no longer fits the up-leveled version of yourself you are becoming.

• Fear not your difficult feelings as it is always out of darkness we are reborn. Meet yourself with compassion. Be like the pupa and retreat to your chrysalis to reflect and redevelop. It is alright to retreat, and more than okay to reinvent yourself when you take in information that expands your worldview and self-concept.

• Celebrate the beauty you are. Be like a butterfly and stretch your wings. Create. Play. Soar. Know you are a stunning work of the Divine. You are free to fly.

May this medicine serve you in your highest self, beloved.

About the Author

SAFRIANNA LUGHNA

Safrianna Lughna, aka the Queer-Spirit Guide, is the founder of Living LUNA, a brand centered around nurturing authenticity, loving without shame, and "Uplifting the Others" of the world. After spending nearly a decade as a trauma therapist, she uncovered her intuitive gifts as a Quantum Creatrix, intuitive healer, and Divine channel. Safrianna has brought healing to thousands of people through her podcasts, courses, individual services, and rituals.

Safrianna specializes in helping people who want to bridge the gap between trauma and triumph through her coaching and spiritual guidance services. She works best with queer and polyamorous individuals, as well as small business owners with invisible chronic conditions. She hosts a variety of events through her membership programs, complimentary workshops, and personalized rituals.

Safrianna is an international best-selling author, educator, and advocate for LGBTQIA+ and polyamorous rights. When she is not hosting healing events or teaching, she can be found playing games with her polycule, petting one of her many cat children, or stretching her multi-passionate creator's wings.

For more information, you can visit:

LivingLUNAs.com & Safrianna.com

Sacred Moon Circle Membership Community:

https://LivingLUNAs.com/sacred-moon-circle

If you are looking for specific social channels, head to: LivingLUNAs.com/socials

FOUR

Meshaelle Pate

JOURNEY TO THE SOUL

When I became a mother, I stepped back into the familiar role of anticipating all the needs of those around me to keep the peace. Growing up hadn't always been easy, so I learned to expect every-one's mood. It was natural to return to that state when my daughter was born, followed by our son three years later. They became my purpose for living. Anticipating their every want and need felt natural to me. I had shrunk myself again. I was no longer Meshaelle. I was the mother of my children. I was the wife of my husband. I excelled at taking care of everyone else in my life.

Yet, the day comes when you realize they don't need you like they used to. The moment where I am crying on the couch, wondering what I will do with my life if I am not taking care of my family. Was I going to spend the rest of my life waiting to do for someone so I could justify my existence?

. . .

The answer was no. The answer was I was going to start taking back my identity. I would look in the mirror and get to know the stranger I had been for the last 20 years staring back at me.

I was going to reclaim Meshaelle.

I was ready to start my journey of connection. I decided I would dig into myself and start healing.

I enrolled in a certification program. It was a nutrition program that dealt with the science, mindset, and spirituality of nutrition. Once I was certified, I took the risk of signing up for the school's live event in Los Angeles. I was 45, and it was the first time I had ever gone away by myself. No girlfriend trips. No self-care time away. Attending the conference would be my first time leaving my family for a weekend, and I had my most embarrassing moment.

I started that Friday morning in Los Angeles in a usual mom way. My son needed help. These were the moments I felt most valued. My day began with a call at 4:30 in the morning when my son called to say he couldn't find his wallet. It didn't matter that I was 1400 miles away and two time zones behind him. I was determined to help him as if I was still home taking care of everything. I walked him through all the places I would typically search for his wallet. He was able to find it in time to go to school. I felt validated. I also felt guilty because I wasn't home to help, and my son was stressed. Mom guilt hit me hard because I had *chosen* to attend this conference. I had decided to leave my family at home. I had no idea I would have a life-defining moment just a few hours later.

.   .   .

I walked into a room full of round tables and strangers. Where was I going to sit? Not in the front of the room. Yet, I also didn't want to hide in the back. I had paid to be here. I owed it to my husband to do it right. I needed to find that perfect spot. The one table that no one else had claimed. That way, I didn't have to be told they were holding it for someone else and had to walk away from the table embarrassed. I had to find a table to welcome others to join me. I could play hostess and meet everyone. My table quickly filled up, and the weekend of learning and working on my business was about to start.

The first speaker stood up, and he was a well-known marketing consultant in the holistic health space. He was teaching us how to market our business. My business school education was coming back, and I was diving in. Yes, mission statements and marketing plans. The presentation was excellent. My brain was all over this material.

Then the second speaker was the founder of the school. She told us her story of going from rags to riches. She spoke on the need to identify and conquer our limiting beliefs. I was following along, and all was good. I was confident in myself because I didn't identify with the limiting beliefs she was highlighting. My day had started early with being needed. I was following along with the marketing infor-mation. My limiting beliefs weren't highlighted, so I felt pretty good. I didn't have to work on anything, so I thought. To be clear, I have since had to work on every limiting belief she mentioned. I just wasn't aware of them at that time. She finished her presentation and put up a slide with a quote from Ram Dass.

"Only when I know who I am will I know what is possible."

. . .

I looked at that quote and realized she wouldn't say anything more. She just asked for any comments we had and was about to end her presentation. The room got still. The Earth might have stopped spinning. I felt frozen while I stared at the screen. Wasn't she going to tell us how to know ourselves? I don't remember doing it, but I raised my hand. They brought me a microphone, and someone with a camera came over. I wanted to say never mind, but I couldn't. Instead, I stood up and asked, "What if **that** is your limiting belief? What if you don't know who you are?"

Then I broke down. The tears flowed, my chin quivered, and I hit my seat hard. I had just confessed to a room full of strangers that I was unsure who I was.

To my left, one table back, was the marketing guru I could only dream of working with one day. There were graduates in this room with podcasts and books and successful businesses. Then there was me, with mascara running down my face while my chin and voice quivered to proclaim that I had no idea who I was to all of them.

The room became hushed. No one else had any questions or comments. All the eyes were on me as I cried and tried to figure out where that comment had come from. My mind wasn't asking it. I *knew* who I was, didn't I? How could I be 45 years old and not know who I was?

Standing up was the most embarrassing thing I have ever done. Yet, it was the most freeing also. I had admitted out loud in front of a room full of strangers that I had no idea who I was outside my roles:

I was a mother and had given everything to that role.

. . .

I was a wife and cheerleader to a fantastic man.

I was a daughter with a rocky relationship with both parents.

I was clear on my *roles* in life, but I had no idea who I was. Fortunately, my story doesn't end with me crying uncontrollably on that Friday afternoon. My brain could not provide the answers I was seeking at this point. I had been trying for most of my life to figure out how I mattered and who I was, yet my brain only provided ambiguity. I realized that the answers I wanted had to come from my soul, not my brain. I had to learn how to connect to my soul.

We are all a soul having a physical experience. We are more than just this physical experience. The world is more than what we have seen and experienced. The entire spiritual world is waiting to help us live to our full potential. We have the entire Universe in our cheering section!

All I needed to do was go inside. Wait, how do you do that? I had never learned that the answers were within us. Or that the loving Universe and all the unseen energy were there to support us.

I had to do three steps to connect to my soul.

1 - Process my emotions.

2 - Learn to trust myself.

3 - Accept my worthiness.

. . .

Process my Emotions

My heart has caused me pain. How can I trust something that has caused me pain? The journey is back to how we were before the heartaches, the letdowns, and the exhaustion of life started.

The journey back to our soul is to answer why we decided to be born into this world at this time.

What is our soul's purpose for this lifetime?

Everyone has their unique reason for that decision. Mine was to help women connect to their souls so the divine feminine energy could rise in us. To be a Warrior for Harmony. Harmony from within will create the peace we all desire in this world.

"As above, so below, as within, so without, as the universe, so the soul..." —— Hermes Trismegistus

My soul had processed the past childhood hurts and 45 years of living. My mind hadn't processed all these hurts. My body was holding onto the energy of these past emotions. I held onto these past emotions as armor against future hurts. Or so I thought!

Holding on to past heartaches doesn't prevent future ones. All this does is cause us to hurt daily. When we don't process the emotions, they are like splinters that we constantly hit and cause us to feel pain. If I held onto my past heartaches, I could create a fortress around my heart, right? That would be the answer to not getting hurt. I would have such a wall around me that nothing could get through. That's exactly what happened. Nothing got through. I didn't feel joy. I didn't feel happy. When something happened to hurt me, it would overwhelm me because it added to the pain I felt daily. Emotional pain is a part of life, unfortunately. Learning to deal with it is more critical than preventing it. When we process our emotions, we feel them briefly, and then the pain is gone. When you first start to process emotions, it can feel overwhelming. Feel free to cry, scream, yell, or punch a pillow if necessary. Just allow yourself to process that you are hurting vs. pushing it down. Processing your emotions is the best way to minimize future ones.

It's safe and healing to do this. Please don't dwell on the emotion; acknowledge it and release it. I had to dig into why I felt specific hurts and then release them. I could not step into who I was born to be when constantly burdened by feeling rejected. Rejection was an emotion I knew well after my parents divorced when I was five. It was how my mind processed my dad leaving. He was still active in my life, but I felt rejected when he left. Fear of rejection was a theme in my life for years. No matter how stable my marriage was, I feared my husband's rejection for years. My fear was projecting onto him. I couldn't stop that fear until I cried for the little girl who watched her dad leave. After I processed that emotion, I stopped having nightmares of my husband rejecting me or fearing he would leave me every six months. The first step I needed to connect with my soul was processing the feelings I bottled up.

Learn to Trust Myself:

How do you learn to trust yourself?

. . .

I began to listen to my internal nudges! Learning to trust yourself is the step where intuition starts to awaken.

Let's do a quick exercise that my coach and mentor, Dr. Ashlee Greer, taught me. Please read all the steps and then close your eyes and repeat them.

1. Quiet your mind. Allow yourself to let all the to-dos and worries of the day go. You can pick them back up in 5 minutes if you want.

2. Ask yourself a simple YES question. Does the sun rise in the east? Is my name _____? Is my birthday in the month of _____? I love _____.

3. Where in your body did you feel the answer besides your mind? It could be your stomach, right arm, or heart; there is no wrong answer. If you need more clarification, repeat the questions. The key is to make it something you don't have to think about. You know the answer and can feel it in your body.

4. When you know where you feel this in your body, you know where your YES center is!

5. Now, let's find your NO center. Ask yourself obvious No questions. Is an alligator white? Do I love traffic jams? Do vacations suck? Whatever is a no for you, ask it!

6. Where do you feel your Nos?

· · ·

Although this exercise is easy, it's crucial. When I found my intuitive yes and no, I didn't have to rely on my brain for an answer. I could start to trust my body more than my brain. Our brain is incredible but has all our life experiences and conditioning, so it does not always provide the most accurate answers. Our subconscious filters our reality. We see things through the filter of our past experiences.

Have you heard of limiting beliefs? These are subconscious interpretations of past events. There are a lot of limiting beliefs we box ourselves into believing. One for me that I am breaking as I write this is that I'm not a writer. Writing has always been something I have avoided and hated until now. My belief that I am not a writer has limited my reaching out to others and how I show up on social media. It has *defined* my life. My spiritual journey made me realize it was time to break through this limiting belief, thus accepting the challenge to write this chapter.

Trusting yourself is also about validating yourself. When we always ask others what we should do or how we should do it, we trust them more than we trust ourselves. Our soul work is ours alone. We learn to validate ourselves when we listen and hear from our souls.

Accept my Worthiness

You do not have to do anything to be worthy of your spiritual connection. You can't earn the approval of your guardian angels. They already approve of you!

The physical world tells us we must earn our way to whatever we want.

· · ·

Make your parents happy so you can have dessert.

Make good grades so you can achieve your scholarship.

Work hard so you can earn a raise.

Our work determines our worthiness in our physical realm.

In the spiritual realm, our existence determines our worth. The fact that we exist at this time is all we need to do to be worthy of the love of the spiritual world.

Our desires, wishes, and wants are all crucial to the Universe. All we have to do is claim them.

The mindset shifts that have to happen to accept your worthiness are essential. What do *you* feel you have to earn? Please make a list of them so you can start shifting them.

Learning to accept my worthiness was a challenge. The first time I heard I was worthy from my spirit guides, I sat on a beach in Florida journaling. I love the peacefulness of the beach. Listening to the waves aligns my soul in a way that is hard to find elsewhere. The knot inside me comes undone, and I'm at peace. I had had a few experiences with channeled writing. My guides took over my pen and wrote what I was hearing from them. I had written that I was worthy when _____ and was working to fill in the blank. For example, I am worthy of vacation when I have made x dollars in my business. However, my guides didn't want me to write anything else.

I wasn't allowed to fill in the blank. They started to write on my paper: you are worthy. My mind kept trying to finish the sentence, so my guides began to put a period. I am worthy. My brain struggled, but my soul got loud and said, "You are worthy because you exist!" That's it. I didn't have to earn my worthiness. All I had to do was accept that I was worthy.

Let's go back to that day at the conference. After the hush lifted, everyone had a suggestion for me. I don't remember them because I only wanted to leave that room. Fortunately, it was lunch break. I bee-lined it back to my room, but only after enduring more stares in the hallway and elevator. My mascara made me look like the sad clown at the circus: two black eyes and marks down my cheeks. I wondered why I had not bought waterproof mascara.

I finally made it to my room and lost it again. I cried more. How had I just let my mask of confidence fall in front of all those I admired? Oh, my brain was beating me up at this point. Yet, my soul was coming alive. My soul had led me to stand up, and it would no longer be quiet. I cried a little more at that realization.

There was one more decision I had to make that day. Do I return to the conference or hide in my room for the weekend? Almost every part of me was voting on hiding. I could sneak out of the hotel and explore LA for the weekend. I could change my flight and head home. My family needed me, right? I had just helped my son that morning. However, I decided to return to that room full of strangers who knew my deepest secret. I left my room, headed back down that long hallway to the elevator, and pushed the button for the conference floor. Staying on the elevator was my last opportunity to run. Once the doors opened on the second floor, I would be in front of all those people again. Would they laugh at me? Laughter would be more acceptable than if they rejected me and acted like I didn't exist. How would they react to my true self? The Meshaelle without a mask of confidence or self-assurance. I was about to find out.

The elevator doors opened, and they smiled at me. Those I had met briefly quickly came over to me and hugged me. I was in shock! They hadn't rejected me. They came to me. I was able to go back to my seat and breathe. I had walked back into the room of strangers, the marketing guru, and the successful business owners without collapsing. I had walked in a more authentic me. I showed my vulnerability and survived. I had let my walls down, and I was alive.

My journey into my soul began in earnest that day. I admitted I did not know who Meshaelle was. I knew who I was as a wife. I knew who I was as a daughter with a less-than-ideal relationship with both parents. I knew who I was as an all-consumed mother. Yet, I had never stopped to ask who Meshaelle was.

That answer hasn't been instantaneous, but it has come as a surprise. I am a deeply connected soul-led woman on a mission to help other women connect to themselves at a soul level so they can live a life that brings them peace, joy, happiness, prosperity, and fulfillment. I now know what is possible, at least for me, because I got to know myself. My possibilities will expand as I dig and value who I am. Not just the roles I have. Or the conditioning that tells me who I am. I have infinite possibilities because I still have more to discover about my soul and its journey. I am excited to keep discovering myself because it unlocks greater possibilities as I do so.

"Only when I know who I am will I know what is possible." - Ram Dass

About the Author

MESHAELLE PATE

As a Soul Alchemist, Meshaelle Pate has a unique approach to helping her clients awaken their spiritual power and live a more connected, fulfilling, and purposeful life. She combines her practical knowledge and life experiences with magical certifications, such as Akashic Records and Reiki, to give her clients a holistic and personalized approach.

Meshaelle's background in Accounting and Information Systems Management allows her to offer practical advice. At the same time, her spiritual gifts help her clients connect with their inner selves and explore their true purpose in life. Combining both aspects, Meshaelle provides a comprehensive approach to spiritual coaching that helps her clients profoundly transform their lives.

Meshaelle values spending time with her family, including her husband and two adult children. Being a "Nani" to two grandsons brings her joy. She enjoys traveling and spending time at the beach. Playing pickleball and possibly taking up golf are also exciting hobbies for her.

Find Meshaelle here:

https://linktr.ee/pate

FIVE

Heather Heselton

DIVINE INTERVENTIONS TO SELF LOVE

It was 7:50 AM on a cold crisp sunny Southern California morning. It was a Monday, and I was on my way to elementary school. I was a shy 9-year-old who was afraid of the unknown.

While sitting in the front passenger seat of my family's army green VW bus, listening to the hum of the motor, I watched my mom across from me concentrating on her driving. I had a tight squeeze on my white stuffed bunny. I stroked its long fluffy ears. It meant a lot to me because my dad had given it to me as a gift when I visited his house in Carson City, Nevada, in the summer before my 3rd grade year. Through the car window, I watched gray building after gray building zoom past, the knot in my stomach grew, and my heart started to race as our destination came into view.

We pulled up to the school and parked. Mom and I entered my 3rd grade classroom, as we did so many times before from the beginning of the year, but this day was different... I was different. I began to panic and thought to myself, "She can't leave me!" As the tears started streaming down my face, I begged her, "Please stay Mom! Please stay Mom!" She was receptive to my distress and stayed in the classroom, and she sat at the desk right behind me. She stated that she could only stay about fifteen minutes because she had to go to work at the university. I sat there paralyzed in fear–the fear of being abandoned. The time came for my mom to go, and I knew I needed to let her leave. As she sat up to give me a kiss and hug to say goodbye, she gave me words of encouragement and said, "You've got this," and walked out of the classroom. The tears continued to stream down my face and I watched the classroom door slowly close as the view of my mother vanished.

The morning seemed to go by so slowly. I wished my mom was still by my side but I knew I had to get through this day alone. When the recess bell finally rang, I stood by the playground fence veering out to an empty lot beyond the enclosed structure where kids played. I stood there squeezing my fluffy white bunny endearingly, and bawling my eyes out so loudly, just wishing that my dad lived with me in my house, instead of in another state. My parents divorced when I was two years old, but it felt like yesterday. I felt so alone on this day. My heart hurt and I felt like I had no hope. I didn't know how to manage these feelings. My heart felt like it was being ripped out of my chest. I didn't know what to do with all of this. I was just a 9-year-old kid and so confused. My mom didn't really discuss the reasons why they divorced and communication wasn't her forte with us kids. I sat with these feelings until they subsided, if only for the day. I wanted to shut these terrible feelings out and never feel them like this again.

That day I subconsciously decided to make a commitment to myself that I would shield my heart, stay separated from myself because it was too painful to hold all those feelings inside of me and never go inside again!

· · ·

When my parents divorced, my mom moved in with my grandparents in Southern California, and my dad stayed in the house I was born in, in Carson City, Nevada. I had no memories of the divorce. I know my mom felt abandoned by my dad, and somehow through my mother-daughter emotional transference, I felt her pain. Children are sponges. We watch our parents and how they live their lives around us. Mom would withdraw and hide her feelings, but I could feel her pain in my body, and in the absence of my father, the void was shattering.

In the Winter of 1981, a new chapter was being written in my family's story. My world had been forever altered: with my dad's departure but now mom bringing someone new into our lives. Mom had found someone special and they were soon to be married - but I couldn't help feeling like something inside me wanted to keep us from starting this next step together. After Dad went away it felt like another part of him had been taken from me; now an unfamiliar man would enter our lives. As I sat there contemplating my mom's new relationship, an all too familiar feeling resurfaced within me. The feeling of being abandoned yet again. I couldn't help but wonder if my mom's new partner would take up all her time and leave me feeling ignored. It's a painful feeling that I thought I had moved past, but here it was back again.

I didn't say anything about these feelings to my mom.

The unconscious memory that I made to myself that day on the playground to stay separate from myself to not feel and show any emotion was in motion; I stuffed it down and forged on.

As a teenager and young adult, I continued to keep myself separate from the world until life-changing events occurred: becoming a mother to my two stunning daughters. My girls were my source of inspiration to start this journey back home to self-discovery and awareness. Divine intervention was at play as well. It was enough to knock the wind out of us as Arizona's sunshine bathed our family with understanding rays that afternoon.

On a sunny September afternoon in Arizona, I was blissfully nursing my beautiful newborn daughter when it struck me that something wasn't quite right: she couldn't latch properly and had little energy to feed. Her diaper had gone dry hours before and she seemed to be losing color, her skin taking on an almost yellowish hue. We soon learned that our precious infant would require open heart surgery only two weeks into life on Earth!

My mom and sister were visiting from out of town and staying at my house. I walked into the kitchen where my sister and mom were cooking lunch. I sat down at the table with them and said, "Something is not right with Makenna. She is not eating." My sister, who was my strength, said, "You need to take her in now!" It was a Saturday and I was afraid no one would be available. My sister's voice inside my head gave me strength to call the doctor. I was able to get into a lactation nurse who was available until 2 PM that day; I quickly got dressed and rushed in a state of panic, desperation, and hoping to get the answers I needed from the nurse. In the examination room, the lactation nurse did the routine checkup to see what was going on, and all of a sudden she looked at Makenna's upper lip. It was pale blue. Makenna was not getting enough oxygen in her system. The lactation nurse made some calls and we were rushed to the ER. The doctors took Makenna in an instant and they ran into an ER room. I called my husband right away and he sped down immediately to meet me at the hospital. As I waited for my husband to arrive, I sat in horror. What was going to happen? What is wrong with my beautiful Makenna? I was trying to hold it all together, and I was clearly in shock. The doctors started doing tests on my daughter; so many I couldn't even count. I stood there watching and I couldn't take her crying anymore, so I walked outside. To see her suffering was so heart-wrenching. I couldn't even breathe. My heart felt like it was broken. *What is happening? Am I going to lose her?*

I took some comfort in calling my family just so I didn't feel so alone; meanwhile, my husband had arrived and was in the room with my daughter while they were doing tests.

I found the courage to go back in the room with my husband and daughter. "The doctors have found what is wrong," he said. "It is her heart! Her main aortic valve is being pinched and can't get adequate blood flow to her heart and her organs are shutting down, time is crucial, they need to stabilize her now!" I couldn't believe what I was hearing! My mind and body went into survival mode and we did what we had to do to save her. The hospital air-evacuated her to Phoenix Children's Hospital.

A nurse guided my husband and me to a hospital room in the ER and there we sat on one of the hospital beds, holding each other so secure, so tightly, and hysterically crying. I couldn't even catch my breath; we couldn't believe what was happening to all of us.

After a week of tests, and trying to stabilize my daughter, her vitals were stable enough to schedule her open-heart surgery.

As I prepared for Makenna's surgery on September 15th, a day that would also have been my Grandpa Ken's birthday had he still been with us, it felt like an unexpected hug from the beyond. Having her name—Makenna—so closely connected to his (her nickname was Kenna) made me feel comforted and reassured knowing we were never truly alone. We remember him in all of life's joyous moments but this beautiful moment was one where faith was especially strong– believing strongly that Grandpa Ken accompanied our every step throughout this process.

The sun had just begun to peek through the horizon when I left my home one morning on my way to the hospital to visit my beloved daughter. My heart was heavy with fear and hope as I drove. Along the way, I stopped at Starbucks to get my morning coffee. I walked up to the counter and this beautiful brown-eyed woman with short brown hair asked me what I wanted to drink. As I looked at the board to choose my hot drink she asked, "Are you doing OK?" I held her gaze trying not to cry. I had always kept my feelings close to my heart but she felt so safe to share myself. The feelings poured right out of me. I shared what was going on with my daughter and she asked me to come sit with her at a table. As we sat down, she looked at me and said, "My daughter had the same exact surgery on her heart ten years ago but she didn't survive. I know what you're going through." I was in awe of the words that were coming out of this beautiful woman's mouth. "I'm so sorry for your loss," I said. She reached for my hand and stared into my eyes. "I'm going to pray for you and your daughter and I'm going to be there at the hospital for you on the day of her surgery! Please give me your number." This woman was a perfect stranger! Her story was the same as mine. This was a miraculous thing that was occurring right in front of my eyes. It felt like an unexplainable coincidence, one that would forever be etched in my memory! As someone who had vowed never to let anyone close again or depend on them for anything, opening up seemed unimaginable until this chance encounter reminded me of the power of true connection and love. I was torn between my commitment I made so many years ago to stay separate and my deepest self.

. . .

But this, what was occurring at this table, in a Starbucks coffee shop felt so good. To receive love and support to let someone show up for me and to hold space for me. It was so foreign to me yet I wanted more. I gave her my number, and she did come on the day of my daughter's surgery to sit with me and support me. I was forever grateful for her presence. She was my earth angel.

With such compassion shown towards a complete stranger, I knew then what genuine kindness can bring into our lives if it is given room enough to grow!

Makenna's surgery went outstanding! She was my little fiery redhead, a fighter!

Makenna's heart was pumping and working properly. I'll never forget right before the surgery the surgeon came into Makenna's room, sat down beside me, and said, "I will take care of her like she is my own daughter." I cried as he gave me a little hug. I felt his sincerity and caring in my soul.

When hardship seemed to come from all sides, I was filled with a deep sense of despair. I had hit rock bottom. But little did I know that the darkest moment before dawn would be one day marked by miraculous interventions: my daughter's air-lifted being just the start! From there on began an incredible journey showing me time and again that we are never alone. When it feels like everything is against us, something far greater awaits beyond. When the Universe, God, Source brings struggles, the shift happens. I've loved this quote ever since: "When shit happens, the shift happens."

· · ·

Makenna's recovery was nothing short of miraculous, and in an instant, it shed a whole new light on my world. I felt like there must be something greater out there that sought to reach me and awaken the depths within myself from which so much had been dormant for just too long. Unfortunately, this moment passed quickly as I tucked away these feelings until another time came around again.

Makenna's miracle opened my eyes on my perspective of being alone and keeping myself separate. It was a miracle for all of us! Maybe I really wasn't as alone as I thought I was. Maybe there was something bigger out there trying to get my attention, trying to wake me up out of my unconscious behavior and stories that had controlled me for so long. After Makenna was better, I reverted down the road of staying separate from myself again, and my focus was now on my daughters. Additionally, the surgery threw me into hyper-anxiety since I had to keep Makenna alive and safe. I became a helicopter mom to make sure everything was perfect!! And never left her side.

One morning, while getting ready to take the girls to preschool, I experienced another powerful divine interruption that forever changed my life.

The girls and I had just finished peanut butter pancakes with syrup, which was a family breakfast tradition that I had for breakfast when I was little. I glanced at the time and realized we were running late for school. I hurried the girls along to finish our morning routine so we could get out the door. My older daughter Jadyn had just turned four years old. She was so sweet, kind, sensitive, with big doe eyes that could look right through you, and a true lover of all things. To this day she is a dreamer, a dancer, and an artist. Jadyn has always felt music in her body. At three, when she heard Mozart's, she said, "Mom I feel so sad with this song, can you turn it off?" She was so in tune with others' feelings and energy since the day she was born. I knew she was sensitive at the time, but I had an agenda that morning. I was corralling the girls to the door to put on their shoes. Jadyn was in her daydreaming state and was taking her time, as she always did. But I was in full panic and helicopter mom mode.

I yelled at Jadyn, "Put your shoes on!" I said it with a stern expression on my face, just how my mother used to look at me. In that moment, time slowed down as she stood there with wide-open eyes, fear etched into every feature of her face. This feeling pierced my soul; it felt like I was somehow hovering above myself watching the replay unfold before me. My sweet little girl's expression shook me deeply and caused a surge of self-reflection: who had taken over here? Had I become just like my mother? How could this happen?! I don't want to parent like this! I need help!

Even though the intensity and shame subsided eventually, this experience awakened my awareness of my patterns and my beliefs that kept me separate. After many years of burying my true self, I felt a stirring inside. To uncover this part of me and discover who I truly was meant to be; it inspired me to seek help beyond traditional therapy sessions that did not meet all my needs. It seemed like the answer lay in holistic healing: letting love and light into those neglected spaces within myself so that I could feel more balanced, connected with core values and dreams as well as tap into true self-love.

It took me some time to figure out that emotions that are triggering for us come from relationships with others and emotional states can be transferred to others through the emotional transference of our feelings, leading people to experience identical emotions unconsciously. These are patterns that have been passed down from generation to generation.

. . .

When we reach rock bottom, we're forced into an existential crisis: are we going to stay down here? Or are we going to find a way back up again? Will we continue letting ourselves be defined by our pasts? Or will we learn how to move forward with all the lessons we've learned so far? When it feels like everything is falling apart around us and there's nowhere left for us to turn, where do we go?

But when we're there, it pushes us to face our patterns, to do the hard work of healing and learning how to take care of ourselves. We open ourselves to find new perspectives, new ways of being. Because the way we have been doing it isn't working for our soul anymore.

Understanding patterns in our emotional states is essential to navigating our interactions with others. Patterns that have been passed down from generation to generation can create complex patterns of emotions, patterns that are often difficult to understand and identify without proper guidance. When patterns are identified and understood, we can begin to recognize the patterns that cause us discomfort or distress, as well as patterns that bring us joy and contentment. Through understanding patterns, we can learn how to move forward in life with a greater sense of self-awareness. This allows us to make healthier choices that promote our well-being, rather than staying stuck in patterns of unhealthy behaviors or attitudes. By digging deep into our own patterns, we open ourselves up to new perspectives and possibilities for growth and transformation. We are encouraged to be mindful of our patterns and the emotions they evoke so that we can better understand and meet the needs within ourselves.

. . .

Learning to meet what needs attention in ourselves is the first step in the path of transformation and self-love. What we think of as habits, addictions, and patterns of behavior stem from years of thinking the same way about ourselves and our circumstances.

With heightened self-awareness comes an opportunity for self-compassion: opening up room to understand ourselves without judgment and realizing that nothing is permanent or predetermined. Making a conscious attempt to look differently at emotions opens a changeful space where entrenched negative patterns can finally dissolve. This allows refocusing toward healthier emotional capacity. It's here we discover we can challenge ourselves to block pattern responses, react with forgiveness rather than shame and understand rather than criticize. This is how our old injuries earn their healing while cultivating wisdom in the heart!

Consider the journey an exploration. Take the time to determine what matters to you and how you want to live your life. Make sure you go beyond simple surface observations; deep dive into your core values and dreams. Only then can one truly become aware of their needs, something that has the potential to unlock so much potential in our lives.

Start by listening to the voice in your heart; know that you are worthy and strong. Celebrate all of the special features about yourself and give yourself permission to grow. Respect yourself, treat yourself with loving kindness, allow your unique gifts to shine! And remember, listen to the stillness within and be steadfast in your pursuits.

Claiming your power is essential to living an authentic life. Coming back to who you truly are, regardless of what life throws at you, gives you an intoxicating feeling of invincibility. When positively channeled, powerful resources can only empower you further in all aspects of life. The most sacred thing you can do is come home to your truest self and honor your authentic journey.

Self-love is not selfish, it is necessary!

Self-love is always available for you, it never runs out, and you cannot use up all of your self-love at once.

We all want to love ourselves, but how do we get there?

Finding the right path might seem intimidating but it doesn't have to feel that way. Together, we can explore different ways of connecting with our true selves and redirecting our thoughts down a healthier path. It all starts with understanding what self-love is – not just the good bits but recognizing the difficult parts too. With this newfound insight into our deeper feelings and needs, we'll gain a better sense of what throws us off balance and how to stay afloat during those moments of insecurity and anxiety. It also involves building trust in ourselves and owning every thought, every decision both big or small, and knowing that these choices will eventually bring us closer to where we absolutely need to be: in tune with our mighty, human selves!

Our life journeys are full of experiences that bring us closer to who we are. Nothing in our lives is ever a coincidence when divine inter-vention presents itself. We can take comfort in knowing that all of the darkness, struggles, and fears will eventually give way to personal growth and healing. This allows us to awaken certain parts of ourselves that have been dormant for so long, obtaining greater clarity on our purpose and path. Our faith sustains us through it all, reminding us that there is always light at the end of the darkest tunnels.

You were made to be radiant. To shine in all the unique ways that make you, you. Far too often we fail to recognize our true magnificent selves, so take a moment and appreciate the beauty of who you truly are. You possess a greatness that knows no limits; let your truest self take the lead on this journey called life, and watch yourself marvel at what comes next. Embrace your soul authentically and wholly— you have the capacity to achieve so much more than you know!

Guided by divine interventions, I embarked on a journey of self-discovery and healing. What started as self-inquiry, self-awareness, and self-love has now become part of my life's mission: to help others uncover their own innate spiritual self. As I present them with the resources to challenge their patterns, and belief systems and gain a newfound self-understanding, so too, do I guide them in unlocking their full potential in order to live their most fulfilling life possible. To me, it is a privilege and an honor to be part of this process for others in discovering who they really are!

About the Author

HEATHER HESELTON

I love helping others connect with their brilliant beautiful selves.

It took many years for me to understand something...

Healing my relationship with myself...

my true self

my whole self

my wisest self

...is the key to healing and building beautiful relationships with everyone and everything in my life.

For many years I lived with what seemed like two versions of me— the one I shared with the world and the one that had secret dreams I didn't think anyone would understand or embrace. I have worked with many people over the years who feel the same.

My journey of coming home to myself involved diving into holistic forms of self-healing—meditation, embracing my psychic gifts, and life coaching.

I've been guiding others home to themselves for almost a decade. It's my honor and privilege to hold space for people as they discover their authentic selves. I love witnessing the transformation that occurs when someone realizes they have everything they need within them all along.

My educational background includes Integral Coaching Certification Program at New Ventures West, Clairvoyant Certification Program at Aesclepion Psychic Training Center. I bring a lot of love and intuition into my work with clients. My hope is that through our time together, you will feel seen, heard, and held in the most compassionate way possible. You are not alone on your journey – let me walk with you for a while.

Everyone is here for a unique reason.

Mine is to help beautiful souls connect with
their most radiant selves so they can finally...

live free!

Find Heather here:

https://www.heatherheselton.com

https://instagram.com/heather_heselton?igshid=YmMyM TA2M2Y=

https://www.facebook.com/profile.php?id=100007181716336& mibextid=LQQJ4d

SIX

Tamara Childs

A MYSTIC'S JOURNEY INTO LIGHT

When I think of Soul Alchemy, it reminds me that life itself is metamorphosis. From our beginnings up to now, tragedy and transition are designed to bring us into self realization.

I believe we are born onto this earth out of our soul's curiosity to be, know, and have more of itself. The process we call "life" forms us in layers like a paper mâché sculpture. Each event is a dip of the paper and it's glued on. You are the being beneath the sculpture. Yet, imagine yourself wearing a hardened cast of that paper mâché and feeling like your lungs can't expand. The suffocation is where we notice something isn't a match for our soul.

Much of that layering is imposed from the outside and we are tasked with removing what doesn't fit our true being, what imprisons us, what holds us back, and the unease of holding energies that make our souls suffer.

. . .

It's taken me years to remove false layers and bloom into the person I was meant to be. This, too, is Soul Alchemy; letting a vision your soul has for you lead you out of any prison structures you've been living in. Removing the layers that do not belong on you.

If you see yourself as a piece of living art, you can also see every experience - especially the most painful ones-will eventually combine to create a mosaic of self that is your being! This master-piece is so much more beautiful than the chipped and broken pieces used to create it.

At one stage, I focused on the broken bits of myself, the parts that didn't seem to "work" in this reality. The parts with sharp edges. Whenever I viewed myself and my story as a sharp little piece, a painful memory, I was disappointed and found myself lacking. But when I learned to step back, gain perspective, and see the ART that *I* truly was, it transformed my sense of self-esteem and allowed me to step into a state of blooming.

I'd like that for you if this is where you are too.

Not Belonging

I was always a sensitive, artistic child who felt I didn't belong anywhere. This is partly because I was born out of wedlock and quickly given away. My mother refused to touch me after I was born but instead had the nurses hold me in front of her so she could observe me.

. . .

"You looked so exotic," She later told me. "Like a little Papoose! I had 3 days to look at you and on the last day in the hospital I reached out my finger to see if you'd grab it but you just cried, so they took you away. And I knew I would never see you again, so I ripped up the snapshots the nurses gave me to remember you by, and threw them in the garbage."

My original parents met for a brief affair then parted ways, with much secrecy, and me as evidence that they had crossed racial lines and committed a social blunder. This sounds old-fashioned, I know. But this was the 1960's and mixed-race children were considered taboo.

"I was afraid if I kept you, I'd see your father's face and resent you for it." My biological mother told me, years later when she explained giving me away.

"And I didn't want people to be mean to me for having a black baby," She further reflected.

She leaned in to make a point. "You know, *HE* wanted you to be *ABORTED*! He even tried to get me to take something from a pharmacist friend of his, but I wouldn't do it. *I* thought you were a miracle."

After two months in foster care, I was adopted by a permanent family.

My new adoptive parents were idealistic teachers at a Quaker boarding school in rural New England. There was a farm, with pigs, horses, and milk cows. We drank the raw milk kept in glass mason jars, and my mother made our own butter in a wooden bowl on the kitchen counter. We had fruit trees and fields and lots of woods to play in. The Quaker faith taught humanitarian values. Quakers have a history with the underground railroad which the African slaves used to travel north to freedom out of enslavement.

I was surrounded by kindly Quaker hippies wishing to do good in the world. One of those good things was my adoption. We were a blended family with two boys being my parents' biological children, and they adopted two girls. There was my older brother, then me, my younger sister, and my younger brother.

But I found myself growing up in a family that didn't coddle sensitivities. My white adoptive parents were middle-class intellectuals who believed children should not be shielded from explicit truths.

"Well, black babies were considered less desirable, and therefore easier to get," my father bluntly explained, when I later asked why I got adopted. "So we got you girls."

The sense of Un-belonging along with the social stigma of being mixed race was one of my first messages of being "broken." I was adopted out of foster care, not belonging to anyone, especially myself. This alienation was what made me feel most alone. I found myself in an environment that also didn't ask me how I felt. I had plenty of books that developed me intellectually but was deprived of the essential feeling, deep inside, that I mattered.

Alien, Mystic

．　．　．

Despite having siblings, I felt alien in my family. I was different from everyone else and my adoptive parents did not understand my needs went beyond shelter and food.

First, I was wired to be highly sensitive to both physical stimuli and energy. It was as if a megaphone was attached to my nerves. This complicated matters of me fitting in.

When I tried to express this sensitivity, I was called "temperamental," "difficult," "too sensitive," and "princess and the pea." (My parents loved my talent for art but not the exquisite wiring that creates the artist.)

My adoptive mother would dress me in scratchy striped sweater dresses and knitted tights that irritated my skin. On top of that, I felt quite "other" when I entered elementary school. My olive skin and curly hair stood out starkly in a school full of blond children in the 1970s. Because I wasn't accepted there, I suffered a lot of inner turmoil.

People would constantly ask, "What are you, anyway?" As if I were not just human.

By the time I was five, the tension of constant discomfort inside me was so great I would pee my pants every day in school, adding to my humiliation.

．　．　．

There I'd be, standing in the line to the cafeteria, or trying to hold it for the recess bell, until I couldn't any longer. Then feeling the warm pee rush down my legs, and dreading the moment the other kids would notice. I'd stare at the big white clock against that muddy lime green wall with the second-hand ticking and wish it was time to go home. The everyday unease of attending that school and not being able to explain my aloneness was the essence of my adopted childhood. I had no exit and no soft places to land. I felt stuck in an unfriendly world, uncomfortable clothes, and hearing unkind words, and I began to feel bad inside.

When I got home, my mother would clean me up and tell me to try to do better. But it was a mystery to her why this happened so she couldn't help me solve the core issue of feeling alien.

At the same time I was trying to fit into Kindergarten, my older brother was pulled out of school, leaving me on my own. When he had his at-home chemo shots I'd run screaming through the house, hoping to save him from the pain and terror of cancer treatment. I'd feel his pain as if it were my own but was helpless to stop it.

I was wired to see other people's energy but did not know what to do with this insight. As a young child, I could tell when others weren't being honest, which caused me to blurt out the truth in uncomfortable silence. And sometimes people were hostile when I was able to see things they were doing they wished I wouldn't. I learned to be quiet and observe, but be careful about what I revealed.

Art was my solace- my way of expressing everything around me. As a budding artist, I also drew pictures of past lives- such as the time I lived my life in a dungeon due to speaking out against the mistreat-

94

ment of another woman. I drew a woman in chains, with a rebellious look on her face and long, black flowing hair, wearing a metal cuff on her upper arm, and knew she had been me. The image disturbed my parents so much they wondered if I needed a psychologist. I drew the insides of people, their character. There was beauty in the ugliness and ugly in the beauty. This was seeing energy clearly, beyond the physical.

Family Tragedy

One day while we kids were playing in the house, we realized something was wrong with my youngest brother Timothy. My father felt my brother's stomach and it was hard like a melon, so he immediately called the doctor at Mass General Hospital in Boston. It was the beginning of a difficult road in which my family constantly struggled. The last happy family picture we had at Christmas was when I was age five. And it was the last time our family would be intact.

For the next five years, my home became a Cancer Zone, with both brothers sick, until the eventual death of my younger brother Tim when I was age nine. I was at the next-door neighbor's house at the moment of his death, March 11th, 4 pm. At that moment I was drinking a cocoa the neighbor had prepared for me and I spontaneously drew a picture of a prince riding a white horse up into the universe and stars, looking happy and free.

"Tam, your brother just died. Come back to the house and look at him." My neighbor told me, as I finished the drawing on her velvet couch in her drawing room. We walked a short path between houses in the chilly March wind. The walk took two minutes but it felt like the most important walk of my nine years.

. . .

Before Tim died he'd been tiny, pale, translucent, and bald with a raspy voice and weary dark blue eyes. His limbs were skinny but his stomach was large and round like the ones on starving children in Africa that I'd seen in my parents' National Geographic magazines. I gazed at him dead; a peaceful porcelain statue, and was immensely relieved he was finally gone. His body lay in my parent's bedroom and I asked them to please open a window for his spirit to leave. I could smell his energy remaining as they sobbed and clung to him there.

During those five years, I learned to keep my needs to a minimum, make my own breakfast and lunch, and tried not to ask for anything. At the time, it was an endless schedule of doctor's appointments, my parents fighting, and constant stress. There was little space for me, my art, my future, and my dreams. Tim's death was the final fracture of our family and it remained broken after that.

My childhood taught me to isolate and use my imagination to comfort myself, to make reality seem less harsh. And I decided that I would have to rely on myself in life. That I'd never belong anywhere, or fit in and I'd have to keep my insights of the world around me a private awareness; a secret. I promised myself I'd someday find my path, and with it, happiness. And, I'd find a way to belong.

But the experiences of this early alienation kept repeating like a cycle. Even through life's good moments, I carried this secret sorrow of my past. This led to persistent anxiety, a sense of being ungrounded, and a critical inner voice that never left me alone. I'd trained myself to live on the back burner of my own life, to not matter– even to myself– and to put off my deepest dreams.

. . .

Sometimes I'd feel a glimmer of inspiration to reach for my soul's desires, then feel defeated by my negative memories, followed by a crash and burn.

A Crisis of Faith

My life went further into crisis in the fall of 1988. I was living in San Francisco and had built a modest existence working as a secretary downtown. My bosses were kind, and the work was stable and routine, if a bit boring. I had a few friends but felt a gap in my life as ever before. I was not happy or fulfilled. I did not feel I was living my purpose. I felt dismal and alone, unable to move forward. *It's important to tell you that my soul had whispered to me many times the elements of my path. But due to the noise in my head, I didn't feel worthy. So I kept choosing the wrong things.*

What I'd chosen in my life felt like a denial of my soul. I felt trapped in an existence that had little meaning. The days rolled into months and soon I'd lost my sense of connection to the dream I brought to town. I wasn't born to sit in an office. I was wired to create a vision! I wanted to use my intuitive knowledge as a business and help others create a life they loved. I wanted to write and speak healing words that would impact the world.

I fell into a deep depression. The walls of my studio apartment that once seemed charming to me now felt like a cardboard box. Life felt stale and empty, colorless. I began to shut down and couldn't hear my own inspiration or guidance anymore. I questioned my very existence. I could not imagine any future for myself.

. . .

An awful thought came clearly to my mind: I was not supposed to have been born. *Just as my father had wished.*

During this downslide, I had a recurring nightmare of being in the dark and unable to turn on the lights. In the dream, I'd feel along the wall in my apartment desperate to get the light on, flip the switch, and there was nothing. And then I'd hear a horrible laugh echoing in my head.

One gray rainy San Francisco day, during this existential depression, I sat on my futon couch watching the drizzle against the bay windows. In my heart, I deeply lamented my inability to have a joyful life. I felt truly broken, busted, beyond repair. Damaged from top to bottom. I knew I had no answers so I prayed for help, then I let go.

As I did, I felt a slight pressure on the top of my head. It moved from the crown of my head down into my chest. What happened next is difficult to explain.

Suddenly I turned inside out as if I were a sock puppet.

The world slipped away and I found myself in a vast space, as if my heart were the entire Pacific Ocean. Ripples and currents of ecstasy expanded through me. I witnessed every thought or belief I had about myself rapidly melting like wax off a candle until there was nothing at all but light.

Since I now occupied a space unlike anything I could put words to, there was little to think about. I became aware that I was traveling at great speed through the universe. Where was I? Curious, I noticed I was no longer on my futon couch in San Francisco but immersed in a river of golden light with a powerful current that was going somewhere fast. I was both a distinct droplet but also just a cell within the larger "body" of this river of light.

The feeling was of molten love.

But, as I felt the last bits of my identity dripping away from me, I pulled back.

I knew if I went with the light I would never come back. Yet a part of myself felt I *must* continue on in this life. The current of light, which had swept me up in an instant, respectfully receded, as if reading my thoughts.

I found myself plunked back into my same body. When I opened my eyes, a little bit of sun came across the old bay window as if the rain had begun to clear.

Nothing felt the same. I'd had a miraculous touch with the divine. A piece of me that had been missing the will to live this life as my soul desired had been reinstalled. The jigsaw of my soul, complete. I had been rebooted and reset.

I returned to my life a different me.

My challenges had not been removed. I still had to be an adult and learn to seek my fortune in the world. But the LIGHT had lit me at just the moment my own pilot light was going to extinguish and I knew with all my being that I was not my story nor the layers of what I thought I'd been. *I was not the regret of my birth mother giving me away, I was not my father's wish for me to not exist, I was not the prejudice I faced as a kid, nor the dark and critical thoughts that had run in my mind like a ceaseless tape.* I was a golden droplet in a sea of light, and could never be extinguished, abandoned, or alone. In this light, I certainly did belong.

This out-of-body experience is not something I told anyone about. There were no words. It even feels uncomfortable to write about it here. You see, it was a wordless experience.

The experience had been visceral, more "real" than life itself. But who would understand?

It was not drug induced but a spiritual intervention my soul was calling for.

I was a good student and dutiful daughter raised by intellectual New England school teachers whose strongest "drink" was Earl Grey tea. Drugs did not trigger this experience. Nor had meditation. In fact, nothing I had done earlier in my life earned me the right to experience such existential bliss. It had simply happened to me, inexplicably, one rainy day, when my soul felt weary and I wondered why I'd been born.

Since now you know my story, you know there's a reason my soul felt weary. I had some healing work to do, and everything about my life I'd avoided facing until now had come to a crisis point.

· · ·

Beneath the Burden is a Gift

My Out of Body experience into the light gave me three important lessons that changed my trajectory. Awakening to the truth of me, Clearing the past hurt and layers that covered me, and Activating a new life of intuition, creativity, and happiness. As I began to correctly rewire my energy system and release what didn't serve my highest purpose, life began to be a gift.

You've opened a book about alchemy. Because of your soul's curiosity. Is it time for you to bloom?

You may have noticed you're a receiver of information in an intensified manner. As if you have a megaphone attached to your awareness. Situations that don't bother others, make you feel nervy and activated. You notice what others deny. This awareness drives you crazy because it's one step beyond what others are willing to acknowledge, so there's no validation for what you know to be true. And you're left there holding the bag, holding energy that doesn't belong to you, burdened.

This intrinsic knowing hasn't been easy. There's suffering attached. Life has seemed punishing and unkind, relentless in its obstacles. This has led you to feel a total sense of denial of the existence your soul is calling for.

You seem more emotional than others, and the pain of people across the world affects you deeply. Perhaps you've put yourself on the back burner as a service to those who seem more needy.

. . . .

You often feel bad about yourself, even though you know you are talented and insightful. You may have the ability to see, smell, feel, hear, and know energy acutely.

You are highly sensitive to environments and noise, and feel others' energy to such a degree *you don't always know it's not yours*. You sometimes spend your day trying not to get derailed by other people's nonsense and drama. That's a hard one because you're a healer, a nurturer, a solver of others' issues.

If you're reading this chapter, I have a message for you:

You're more than a nursemaid for others and their angst. Despite the fact, you're wired like a psychic sponge. Just because you feel it, doesn't mean it's yours to hold.

There's a deeper purpose for your being that goes beyond the Cosmic Janitor role you thought you were assigned. Cleaning up energetic debris is not your job. Your job is much more exciting than that and your soul will take you right to it.

You contain a dream that your soul knows all about. You've been waiting for your turn, your opportunity to activate a beautiful life, created by you. Your level of self-knowledge is high, as is your curiosity to uncover any secrets holding you back from this soul vision.

Consider that your soul has decided it is time to be center stage with this vision. No more "being on the back burner." Putting out fires for other people is no longer a sufficient lifestyle for you. Nope.

You're ready to have the life you came here to live, without excuses. Picture that you're wired to bloom and you're prepped and ready to receive the electricity. You're free to choose the next chapter of your life to make it your best.

There are 3 Next Steps that will help this happen.

* If life has tested your faith and left you believing you didn't deserve.

* If tragedy has set limits for you.

* If a cascade of difficulties led you to perpetuate patterns of perfectionism, paralysis, and overwhelm thinking you're unworthy to attain your dreams.

* If asking for what you want and believing you can have it has been a challenge.

* If you've experienced a repetitive cycle of self-denial.

* If life has trained you to say no to yourself to keep someone else happy.

How I transformed in 3 Steps:

Awaken

I received messages about my life that changed my trajectory. I knew I contained a cell of light inside an enormous being of pure love.

I understood the tragic events of my past did not limit my future happiness.

I took back my power from others who had denied me and caused me to feel bad about myself.

I became aware of new possibilities and timelines my soul preferred.

Clear

I forgave the losses of my past, the transgressions, the neglect, and abuse.

I deprogrammed my being of unworthiness and deleted psychic pictures belonging to other people.

I updated my family contracts, ancestral contracts, and agreements with my soul.

I removed all residue of harm done to that 5-year-old and her dreams.

I cleansed negative influences that hovered in my psychic space like smog.

. . .

I corrected my poor self-image to one of love, self-acceptance, compassion, and appreciation.

Activate

I learned to rewire my psychic circuitry so that I could receive higher-level energies.

I accessed my inner wisdom and ability to read the symbolic soul messages alerting me to a correct flow for a better life.

I became the true mystic I was born to be. I learned astrology and honed my ability to see and accurately read energy to determine the best path for myself, and my clients.

I finally listened to my soul and aimed my inner compass toward what makes me happy.

Today my life is full of possibility. I pay attention to my intuition, which guided me out of the concrete jungle of Los Angeles into a quaint town in the Rocky Mountains. As a professional healer, intuitive, and astrologer I devote my time to writing, astrological charting, and assisting my clients with their transformations in my private practice.

Serenity is one of my core values. The natural world offers daily healing, which soothes my highly sensitive system.

Looking out my dining room picture window I see fresh spring snow weighing down the branches of my 120-year-old Spruce tree. My beloved Kelpie, Gracie, sits next to me, calmly soaking up the same vibe, watching me with warm, alert eyes. I feel the joy of living in my bones, now wired in. It is my joy to guide others in first understanding their special unique soul wiring, and then removing the influences of past trauma so they can truly access their own unlimited possibility.

My greatest gain from all my lived experience is now having the joy of choosing where I focus my precious energy and doing that gives me the freedom to create from vision rather than turmoil.

With my psychic insight clear and functional I've been able to guide hundreds of clients toward creating a life of their dreams also. I work in the realm of potential. Any that have been deactivated get to be turned back on!

About the Author

TAMARA CHILDS

Tamara is a professional astrologer and intuitive who specializes in spiritual detox for highly sensitive people. She teaches clients how to remove draining energies and restore dominion over how they feel.

As a popular radio show host, she was known for her razor-sharp insight into how to live in higher levels of joy and purpose.

Tamara also loves the stage and has written many original performances shown in a Los Angeles theater. Her storytelling includes themes of social justice, with a dash of satire to refresh the spirit.

She holds an M.A. from the Institute of Transpersonal Psychology in Palo Alto, California.

Tamara lives near Yellowstone National Park, where the sun is strong and the air is fresh. In winter she's cross-country skiing; other months she's tending her apple trees, baking pies, and having adventures with her Kelpie, named Grace.

Find Tamara here:

https://linktr.ee/tamarachilds

SEVEN

LaArie Yonoel Juinde

(I·DEN·TI·TY) NOUN

~BEcome the person your soul is here to BE. ~

Epic quote from [the book] Who Not How [by Dan Sullivan]:

"The definition of hell is: Your last day on Earth, the person you became meets the person you could have become."

Today, I identify as an extraordinary human. My mission is quite simple: to unite the world. Unite in agreement to seek to understand first, instead of automatically compartmentalizing a label for each human we come in contact with. And of course, labels come with passing judgment.

· · ·

I am committed to doing all the things in my awareness for that last day on Earth. If I do meet the person I could have become, it will be a mirror image of who I was, while here. My intention for you as you read this chapter is for many ah-ha moments that will ultimately become pivotal markers in your life, catalysts, if you will. Do I have permission to speak directly to your Soul Identity? If you agree to proceed, please do so with an open mind and with the intention of forward progress. Proceed with curiosity. Proceed after you have asked your Soul Identity for permission to walk away with the awareness you are here and meant to receive.

I remember the first identity marker given to me by my mother. We were walking along the muddy dirt road on a weekend day in Upper Michigan, or the Yooper as the locals call it. I listened to the waves crash against the beach bank, half-eavesdropping on my mother and grandmother catching up as we were only visiting for the week-end. Walk-skipping on the dirt road up to the "new road" as we call it to get the postal mail. It felt good to be free at Grandma's house.

I couldn't have been more than 3 or 4 years old. My mother called out, "Don't get your Nikes all dirty, they are all sold out and we can't replace them." Very briefly looking down at my feet, seeing my navy blue nylon Nikes, with a white leather checkmark, thinking to myself, *I wanted a girl color, mom wasn't able to get me a girl color.*

It was a VERY popular time for Nike, early 80's and they were all the rage. My mother somehow managed to snag a pair for herself and her four girls. My pair did match my mother's pair, so I was happy we were twins. It made me feel special.

Then as my eyes made their way back up from looking at my new Nikes, I took notice of the light jacket tied around my waist by the arm sleeves. I was quite warm from running free, down the country dirt road, as we lived in the city in an apartment—five females in a 2-bed 1-bath apartment. Many acres, fresh air, the sun peering down on me, I was recharging. It. felt. good.

Just as soon as the thought popped into my mind, I blurted out, "Mommy, can we go swimming?" Laughing during her very fast reply she said, "No, the water is freezing this time of year. You're such a Pisces, always wanting to be in the water, no matter what." She continued to laugh and smile. Curiously, I replied, "What's that?" Thus, my first Astrology lesson. I was told I was a Pisces with Scorpio rising. Or in child terms, I was a fish that liked to sting people.

I remember looking up at my mother's face as she was speaking to me and assessing her mannerisms. She was serious. This was an actual thing. She said it with such conviction and authority. I automatically believed her. My mother was my entire Universe until I was about 9 years old. Everything she said was true. It was a fact. It was so.

She went on to tell me I was a fish and that was why I loved water so much and the Scorpio means Scorpion. I sting people really badly when I am angry at them. That I can hold on to grudges for lifetimes. That I will never forgive people if they double-cross me or if they make me angry. I remember taking it as fact like someone telling you the sky is blue and the grass is green. It just is.

And that was it, the first time I can remember someone gifting me an identity marker, and my own mother at that. Who'd a thunk? Of course, I accepted this identity marker. I quickly internalized it to be a good girl. I *always* listened to my mother.

. . .

Well, reality is, I had just barely escaped with my life a short 12-18 months earlier when at that very same spot my favorite sister had taken me swimming at about two years old and I stepped on the slippery green algae swaying back and forth in a mesmerizing rhythm on one of the rocks in the water. I then fell underwater, face up. I couldn't get my bearings. It felt like a million years of sheer panic. I remember opening my eyes and the bright blue sky was blurry from the water above me. I highly do not recommend looking at the sun underwater; the same situation applies as above water. I flailed underwater trying to get my sister's attention, panicking, not being able to breathe, talk, or scream.

Yet, that near-death experience described above didn't stop me from ever getting back in the water, joining the swim team in 7th grade, or the diving lessons that I took the summer of 5th grade. Or the countless trips to JoAnnie's Pool in the summertime when the great lake was unavailable. Why is that? Let's take a deeper dive.

I had naturally let go of almost dying at the hands of the mighty Lake Michigan in under a foot of water. Why wasn't I holding on to the 'trauma' from that experience? As adults, hold on to the traumatic experiences of events we attach emotion to. We're taught to wear these traumas of badges of honor. (more on this later) Interestingly enough, I hadn't been taught yet. I hadn't been taught to hold on to the traumatic emotion. I had the experience, I let it go and moved on from almost drowning.

As a daughter, a sister, and a granddaughter, I wasn't babied or given special attention when I fell underwater and almost drowned. Not one person in my life attached emotion to it. I was validated, then it was dropped. Not one person unconsciously made or took actions to keep me out of the water or kept me from swimming. I was told to be careful like usual. I was told to stay close to the edge of the lake or in the shallow part of the pool. That was it. I wasn't taught to wear it as a badge of honor that I would be able to identify as a drowning survivor or a victim of Lake Michigan and associate pain with bodies of water.

As a matter of fact, living near water has been a prerequisite for any home we have lived in. If it was an apartment, they had to have a pool or there had to be a lake with swimming access nearby. To this day, I still live near a body of water. Is it because I am a fish, or is it because of an identity marker given to me by my mother? Either way, it isn't a negative identity marker, so I haven't addressed it. I am totally ok with water and I really do love swimming and being by massive energy sources. Love, love, love, the water! Don't you?

I wasn't given an identity marker of "I am not a very good swimmer" or "I can't go back in the water because I almost drowned last time." Like with the astrology lesson, I was told I was a stinging fish and I hold on to grudges for lifetimes. The truth is, I held on to that deep-rooted identity marker of a 'stinging fish' until I was about 35-37 years old. It wasn't until I really dove deep into self-development that I understood, I ***could*** change me. I ***could*** own my own POOP. I was actually in control 100% of the time.

I didn't have to hold all of this anger, resentment, and rage for my entire lifetime. Or subsequent lifetimes. Seemingly, the mainstream matrix teaches us in various outlets to hold on to and/or identify as the survivor of childhood abuse or a sexual assault victim. When these examples internalize the trauma in compartments accessible via triggers or activations we give up our free will. What if someone who has previously identified as such were to change this identity marker to: I just learned about sex at an early age. There's a massive difference in the emotion attached to this statement vs being a victim or survivor. The mainstream collective will have everyone second-guessing everything you believe in when we lack self-confidence and care what others think about us.

When I finally became aware that I didn't have to follow the rigid compartments of astrology, I could change who I identified with as much or as little as I wanted to. I was able to identify as whoever I really wanted to be. I started crafting who I wanted to be and showing up as these new identities. Being fully transparent, I have always done this. I wasn't actually aware of the natural process I had developed. I remember back in 2008, I was reconnecting with a friend of mine from the 90s and I made a statement that I lost 45 lbs in 3 weeks after having my son. She responded by saying, "You were always good at that. You decide what you want and then you get it." What a revolutionary and powerful way to think!

Unconsciously, I hadn't thought about this previously but she was right. I have always decided what I wanted to be, then I became the thing. Whether or not I quit smoking, I changed my identity to a non-smoker. I observed my habits, of when I smoked, what I did before and after I smoked a cigarette. Then, I went to work to identify as the opposite. I chewed gum on my breaks at work. I went on 10 min walks vs smoking. I found a walking buddy to keep the social aspect of the addiction to smoking. I spent the money on something nice for me vs burning up a pack a day. I changed my identity to someone who preferred to smell good, with white teeth and fresh-smelling clothes vs being okay with smelling like smoke. I replaced my smoking habit with working out.

With regard to identifying as a "stinging fish": the stinging portion (resentment, anger, and retaliation) I could simply let it go and Identify as someone who is 'the prize.' Bless and release. Move on with my life. I am committed to blessing the person who wronged me, become accustomed to self-assessment, and owning my part in said event. Letting it go. Also, internalizing an unwavering knowing that it is THEIR loss by not being able to be associated with me any longer. (I am the prize mindset.) And genuinely wishing them the best.

Wholly buckets of SUNSHINE!! Once I took ownership and changed my response to others, my life has fully transformed! I am happier and can sleep at night. I sleep ALL night long! Like a baby! I no longer hold onto grudges for life or at all! It truly opened up a vacuum of a revolutionary vortex in my life. The lives of those around me are also influenced.

Mainstream Matrix Identity: The identity for those in the mainstream matrix *is generally based on feeling emotions and evaluating conditions that are irrelevant.*

When we sit down and really think about the things that are posed as what we should identify as we have been taught to place emphasis and emotion on the wrong identity markers. We have been taught to focus on and place anger on distractions vs what our soul's identity is here for. Identifying as a gender, as a sexual orientation, as a religion, as a color–all of these are great for knowing who you want to be and to solidify an unwavering knowing in the way you show up. However, they do not make or break you.

These. Are. Labels. One of my favorite quotes by **Sören Kierkegaard** reads, "Once you label me, you negate me." When the individual must live up to the label, the self ceases to exist. The same is true of self-labels. You could be negating yourself by identifying with your trademarks, rather than your own potential for growth."

These are the mainstream matrix's way of division and a way of getting you to hold on to your emotions. The mainstream matrix has mastered owning you via your emotional attachment to your trademarks or your own identity markers. The mainstream matrix has mastered humans using their own free will to disqualify themselves and become engulfed in their own self-hatred and depression, so much so that it is crippling them emotionally, physically, and mentally at alarming rates.

For example, the mainstream matrix purports:

• of someone stuck in a holding pattern until they decide it is ok if two people who identify as the same sex are allowed to marry each other. If they are not hurting themselves or anyone else, does it really matter?

• evaluation of I can only associate with people who have the same skin tone as me? Do you want people to see you as the amazing human you are or by your skin tone?

• Wars; mainstream matrix's evaluation of wording information in a way to skew a viewpoint vs seeking to understand first. The mainstream matrix was able to unite almost the entire world of standing in unity with a specific country. However, are they united in standing with a country, or are they united in standing against the 'leader" of the opposing country?

○ If so, what was actually accomplished was uniting the entire world against the leader(s) of the opposing country. The entire country doesn't deserve the hate. Really think about that. The entire population of the opposing country is innocent. They did not authorize war. They did not have failed meetings with other countries. It is the leader(s) of the countries. Not the entire population of the world.

• And my favorite: the mainstream matrix evaluation of not crossing an imaginary line between states with trees that grow together outside without boundaries. I bet those bugs don't adhere to the imaginary lines. Those rebels! (In the Midwest, USA, there is a law that states that wood/trees can not be brought across imaginary state lines. The reasoning is due to the thought of bug cross-contamination. HOWEVER, the bugs and trees grow outside freely without borders.)

Trying to decide the rightness or wrongness of someone else's life is really a reflection of the lack of aligned identity of your own life. As long as you are not hurting yourself or anyone else who cares where you are from? Who cares about the color of your skin? Who cares if you want to be in a same-sex relationship? And for the love of love, who cares if you put chopped wood in a vehicle and travel with it??

Flip the emotions and feelings to BE an extra-extraordinary human, to BE an amazing present parent, BE the person who creates positive relationships, and such. Place emotion and emphasis on your own growth, and your own potential. Remember, when we leave this body, what if we have the opportunity to meet the person we *COULD* have become, yet didn't due to crippling ourselves with self-hatred and fear? What we have been taught to do is invest time, energy, focus on fixing the previously evaluated erroneous conditions. All the while, your very own identity, who you are meant to be, is patiently waiting on your ability to rise above the mainstream matrix and identify as BEing who you came here to be.

• • •

You are an Ultra Premium Superstar! You really are. If you are here **<u>YOU</u>** are an Ultra Premium Superstar! This is one thing I know for certain but you're letting your mainstream matrix ID get in the way. When clients verbalize their transformations, some of which are instant, there is nothing that excites me more than being there to witness their shifts in identity markers.

The world is desperate for genuine leadership. Think about the current leadership we are experiencing in the world today. Do you think there may be some room for improvement? So do your soul's tribe. They are eagerly waiting for you to accept the alchemy your soul has in store for you. Think about your tribe, sisterhood, gentlemen's club, your soul alchemy people who are coded to you just waiting in hopes that you will step into BEing who you came here to be! And if you don't, what won't happen to those who you are here to serve? Who will miss out on massive transformation by you not BEing who you are here to BE? What part of your soul's alchemy is missing out on opportunities, experiences, or even pure love? Go deep and ask.

"Once permission was received from my inner child, that is when the release really happened." -Ultra Premium Client Testimonial

Soul Alchemy for me, is the freedom to choose who you want to be and be it. You have the answers inside of you. When you give yourself permission to allow your soul's identity to come out, allow, and give your soul's identity the permission to be who you came here to be. Allow and give permission to your soul's identity to be the person you could be. Your highest and best. Are you living your hell? Or are you willing to become aware of more satisfaction and less pain? Remember that epic quote from the book, *Who Not How* by Dan Sullivan: "**The definition of hell is: Your last day on Earth, the person you became meets the person you could have become.**"

When we can begin to realize that our differences collectively refine us, then diversity is something that benefits us. Contrarily, when we are diversifying ourselves down to all of our traumas, badges of honor, faults, and discords, we are just strengthening walls that separate us.

This chapter is dedicated to my parents. I want you to know, intentional or not, I have embodied all of the lessons. From the sweet Valentine's Day cards and no birthday cards from my dad. To the angry burnt cups of coffee, my mother would make when having a bad day. I have internalized these lessons. I have forgiven EVERYTHING I held onto as a wild child. I have embodied that you both gave me ALL you had to give. I now know this. I know the things we went without or the ways we lived were lessons I came here to learn. I am grateful my soul chose your parents for the perfect environment to learn and explore diversity. I know these built character and I thank you. I thank you both for your rigid loving ways and they have made me a better human.

I love each of you,

LaArie Yonoel Juinde

——————————————— Disclaimer ———————————————

All content contained in my materials, both personal and general, are entirely my personal knowledge, experience and opinion and are intended for personal development purposes only. These chapters, workbooks, videos and information are not to be taken as medical advice but as spiritual information. I am not, and do not claim to be a medical doctor, therapist or licensed mental health professional. If you have a health problem, please see a Doctor or other appropriate professional. Any information received here should not be used in place of professional medical and/or psychological treatment. You alone are responsible for any of your choices, your decisions and your actions in life. Any use of information included in any of my materials is to be followed at your own risk and know that you are responsible for what you do with the information you choose to receive from this book/workbook or any of my material. All content is for entertainment purposes only and those under the age of 18 should not use this site except with adult supervision.

About the Author

LAARIE YONOEL JUINDE

LaArie is the go-to expert on Identity Linking in her field. She facilitates the linking from the unwanted identity markers to the desired identity markers with her profound Signature 3-step Identity Blueprint program. Her clients experience her and their results as fast as an instant.

What sets LaArie apart from others is the space she holds to play with her clients unlimited potential. In her truly magical world, there is only potent transformation and zero watered-down messages. She has a unique ability to dive deep below being in the weeds of the mainstream matrix, see the end result, and hold that space for her clients in a way that collapses time and space.

LaArie is mission-driven to unite the world in seeking to understand verses automatically judging someone on their visual appearances, their words, or their current identity, keeping the lines of communication open across all genders, races, sexual orientations, religions, countries, or any other new division that may arise in the collective world matrix view.

LaArie enjoys reading, learning new things, horseback riding, keeping up with her own identity, and as you have possibly guessed, all things warm water weather related.

Find LaArie here:

LaArieYonoelJuinde@yahoo.com

https://www.facebook.com/LaArieYonoelJuinde

https://www.instagram.com/laarieyonoeljuinde/

Youtube: @laarieyonoeljuinde8930

EIGHT

Kaitlyn Algar

RELEASING WITH THE MOON

I wiped down the chest fly machine I had been using with disinfectant spray and a white paper towel. I headed to the front of the gym. My throat began to constrict as it did when I was a child when I had something to say, but I was more afraid of how someone would respond than I was about speaking my truth. The lump formed around my voice box and sat.

Ellie was the manager at Move It And Lose It Gym. Generally, I liked her. She was a great people-person. I respected how she took the time to connect with the clients and remembered most of their names. I thought we shared that quality and each valued putting the customer experience first. However, she got word I was looking for other work. A well-meaning client brought flowers in for me as a thank-you and farewell gift. I had spoken with her about my desire to use my health coach certification and help clients on a more comprehensive level. The trouble was I hadn't mentioned my plans to leave to Ellie. I applied to several jobs but hadn't officially accepted any new positions, so I hadn't given my two weeks' notice.

· · ·

Since Ellie got word about my plans for departure she started writing me up about the smallest breaks in policy. For example, working the floor without a shirt tucked in. I worked out with clients as a personal trainer in the gym and did not always notice when my shirt came untucked. She wrote a disciplinary slip for not wearing my name badge. Often my badge would be on my jacket, but I would get warm, take my jacket off, and forget to move the badge from my jacket to my t-shirt. I knew what was coming. I called her higher-up, Stephen, as a last-ditch effort to save myself from being fired. Yes, I was looking for other jobs, but it was because I cared more about client progress and my work as a personal trainer than I did reading a script verbatim when answering the phone, tucking my shirt in, or wearing a name badge. My clients gave Ellie great feedback about our work together; they surpassed their goals time and time again.

A lump sat in my throat now because Stephen had arrived at the gym and I was headed in to talk to him. My chest felt tight. I let out a sigh and dropped my gaze to the floor.

"Listen, I don't know what happened between you and Ellie, but even after today you need something and give her a call, and she will show up," Stephen proclaimed.

As if that could possibly matter, I thought silently to myself.

"We can do this one of two ways," Stephen said. "I can fire you today, or you can write a letter of resignation today and continue to use us as a reference for future jobs."

. . .

124

Words filled my mind, but I did not dare let them escape my lips. I stood up, gathered my things, and made my slow retreat out the front door of the gym. In August 2017, I got fired for the first time in my life.

I felt defeated. The last place I wanted to go was home. I drove to one of my favorite parks I found since moving to Connecticut: Fort Shantok. I parked my car, slammed the door, and marched across the field surrounded by cedar trees. I stepped into the woods; a well-trodden path led downhill. I let momentum take me. I followed a skinny path with grooves in it where rainwater from past storms rushed down to meet the Thames River. My soul too was ready to be washed. I walked down, down, down; it was like something was pulling me to the water.

I met the river and arrived at stillness. I looked out across the water and I let go. I let go of holding my breath. I let go of the fury of mistreatment. I let go of incongruency. I let go of misunderstanding. I let go of holding myself back. I felt the moisture on my face as I sat on a boulder by the river, evidence my tears had streamed down, down, down.

I sat on the boulder, knees pulled towards my chest, and I cried. My inner child cried with me. She cried at the rejection she felt when she found out Miranda, the girl she'd given the necklace with the dolphin pendant that read "BEST" on it had exchanged a tie-dye bracelet that read "FRIEND" to the girl, Rachel, who lived across the street. She cried about the time she didn't make the high school freshman girls' softball team. She cried about the gorgeous hazel-eyed boy, Daniel, who never asked her out. She cried at the two-timing, sleazy, bad boy Nathan, her first love, who said he'd go the movies with her, met her there, acted strange, leaving the movie multiple times, then, when the movie was over, saw him talking to another girl.

The clouds in the sky parted and unleashed sunbeams that streamed down and warmed my face. I lifted my gaze out across the river. I watched the waves move on top of the water and I set the intention for my emotions to move with them. I sat there by the river and thought quietly to myself. I felt proud that I spoke up for myself. I felt proud I did not give in to something I did not agree with. I felt proud of myself for embracing an opportunity to move on instead of attempting to hold on tightly to what once was. With an inhale I sniffled. I took a deep breath in, and I let out a loud sigh. I applied to multiple jobs, but the position I was most excited about was a wellness coach position with a mental health agency. I decided to trust I would get the job I was most excited about. *I'll hear from the employer soon and be invited to an interview*, I thought to myself. *Everything is going to work out. I know what is best for me. While the job at Move It and Lose It Gym was a step up from waiting tables and working customer service in a spa boutique, it wasn't my forever work home. And that's okay*, I thought. I watched the sunlight dance on top of the waves of the water. The bright white light sparked hope inside of me. "It gets better from here," I told myself.

Later that evening, I confessed to my husband Brent my troublesome day. "I am a bit worried," I shared. "I am supposed to go to Texas next week and meet up with Ang and Sam. I really don't want to miss this opportunity to reconnect with them. I'm going to need you to help me out for a while," I told him. I looked into his eyes with a humble expression on my face. Brent looked back into my eyes. He reached down for my hand encircling his warm fingers around mine. "Of course," he said. My shoulders dropped with a sigh. I let the corners of my mouth rise ever so slightly. "Thanks," I replied and dropped my forehead down and forward until it met his shoulder. I leaned in for support.

. . .

"So what are you going to do now?" Brent asked. "I am going to take care of myself," I replied. "I've spent so much time since I moved here running around and working hard." I moved to Connecticut in 2015 after we got engaged in the Spring. "I need to slow down."

I believed I would get hired for the Wellness Coach position at the mental health agency I applied for. I chose to believe. In the meantime, I decided to get to know myself better. The fury and fire of the ego death that occurred when I got fired from Move It And Lose It Gym fueled me to lean into only doing things that I wanted to do. I was fueled to discover my passions. Up to that point, I had listened to others' advice. I worked at jobs that I knew existed. I made money in ways I had in the past. My needs were met, but my passion was not there. Now I had free time and freedom to express my soul in ways I had always dreamt of.

Some days my whole body tensed in fear. Negative thoughts crowded my mind. I planned a girls' trip with great friends I met while studying abroad in Australia for a semester in college. *I don't have a job. How can I go on a vacation?* I asked myself. Yet, I knew what my life was like previously: working waiting tables and checking out guests from their day at the spa. Passionless. I declared I wanted something new. I took action towards it. Now was my opportunity to solidify a new way of being. I acknowledged the fear and the thoughts of working at a restaurant again. I witnessed them and welcomed them to move. Then, I chose to focus my energy on faith. Instead of returning to running around spinning my wheels at passionless jobs, I gave in to my curiosity about what could bring me joy.

. . .

I bought my first tarot deck: the traditional Rider-Waite tarot deck. As a young teenager, I was always drawn to gothic art, Wicca, Earth medicine, tarot, and understanding the Spirit realm. I never dared buy a tarot deck however; people would think I was strange, like one of those goth kids in all black, dark make-up, and weird. I already stood out with my platinum-blonde hair and translucent Irish skin. "She looks like an angel," I recalled hearing my cousin say as she shared with me what an adult in the church family said aloud one day. I grew up Christian, and while my family was not overly strict, I do remember being discouraged from playing with an Ouija board. "Witchcraft is bad. You can invite evil spirits," I heard the words of a distant memory play in my mind.

"F$@* it!" I proclaimed to the Universe. If it is bad, I will know, and then I can stop doing it at that time. I bought my first tarot deck and patiently waited for it to arrive so I could start to learn the meaning behind the cards and the practice of the craft. While researching, Amazon suggested another product I might enjoy: *Moonology* by Yasmin Boland. A deep love of mine that went back as far as I could remember was gazing up into the night sky. I enjoyed the soft depth of darkness and the contrast of the brilliant white stars and Moon that danced together. My heart fluttered with excitement at the opportunity to deepen my understanding of the night sky. I clicked "Add to Cart." I recalled Gabby Bernstein's LIVE. She shared a meditation and promoted her book *The Universe Has Your Back*, and the new exclusive release of the oracle deck *The Universe Has Your Back*, a perfect tool to deepen a spiritual practice. I knew the power of meditation. I found it early on my healing journey when at age 15 I declared I was tired of being overweight and irritated all the time. Meditation was a tool many "happy" people used. I was open to trying it and quickly fell in love with the peace that resonated through my body when I practiced. A soft nudge moved my Spirit, *"how fun would it be to add this to your practice?"* When I watched Gabby Bernstein's LIVE and watched her use the cards something sparked my curiosity. Plus the illustrator of the deck, Micaela Ezra, is from Australia. I studied abroad in Perth, at Curtin University, for one semester in 2012 and fell in love with the country and culture. It warmed my heart to think I could reconnect with the energy of Australia in a fun new way. I added the oracle deck *The Universe Has Your Back* to my cart and checked out.

No longer working a full-time job I gave in to the urge to slow down. The temptation to panic continued to exist–to search for jobs, to return to old jobs, to return to what I knew. I recognized the temptation and I made a new choice. I knew what did not work. I felt ready to explore what might work and what might simultaneously feel good. [I attribute my awareness of this temptation and the ability to make a new choice to my consistent practice of working my awareness muscle, my intuition. Practices like meditation, mindfulness, yoga, exercise, and mindset re-working.] In the mornings I made celery juice and fresh pressed juices. Afterward, I exercised. I often either completed a yoga practice on YouTube or a PopSugar Fitness video on YouTube. I meditated. I leaned into studies of Moonology and tarot. I enjoyed following my curiosity each day. I enjoyed practicing techniques I had never tried before. I felt like a kid in elementary art class. I played with tools and colors and materials creating, turning something into something else.

The day arrived to board the plane and head to San Antonio, Texas, for my girlfriends' getaway. I felt elated thinking about reconnecting with my good friends. We studied abroad together in Perth, Australia, in 2012. We became close adventuring in a new country together. We saw each other briefly at my wedding in 2016, but now we'd have a long weekend to connect and be silly. My energy was simply buzzing as I packed my suitcase. I chatted with my parents on the phone. "Uh, where are you heading again?" Mom asked. "There is a hurricane headed into Texas."

· · ·

Oh God! I just left chaotic energy. I guess it only makes sense that I fly into it, I thought to myself. I checked the weather. A hurricane was set to hit Texas near Corpus Christi. *Well, I'll leave the decision of whether I fly or not up to those who know more about the safety of flying than me,* I thought. My South Node Cancer normally has a tendency to cry over spilled milk and make a big deal about things when they're outside of my control, but I already declared I was choosing a new way. *I'll be notified if the flight is canceled,* I thought. I chose not to worry and finished packing.

My body was buzzing with energy as Brent drove me to the airport. I felt elated to escape with the girls and embody a playful energy again. Wine tasting, dancing, big belly laughing, and walking down memory lane were likely to ensue. I had not connected with many girlfriends yet, since living in Connecticut. Generally, I found the people to be like the winters on the East Coast, cold. I went to college in Kentucky and grew up in the Midwest in Ohio. I was excited to explore the South, hopefully, a slower and friendlier environment, with tasty cuisine.

I jumped, startled by the sound of my phone ringing in my pocket. I pulled it out of my pocket and saw a Connecticut number displayed on the screen. The corners of my mouth slowly lifted into a smile, *could this be....* "Hello," I answered. *It was!* I gleefully shared with myself. United Services, the mental health agency, called about the Wellness Coach position. They wanted to set up an interview with me. I let them know I was headed out of town and when I would return. We scheduled an interview and I hung up the phone. "Yes!" I shouted, throwing both hands in the air. I turned to my husband, my eyes lit up with excitement. "It's all happening. I'm going to get that job as a wellness coach," I said, doing a little dance in the passenger seat. The call to set up an interview felt like a reward for choosing a new way of being and saying yes to my joy instead of overworking myself. "But first things first. It's time to celebrate with my girls," I said to Brent and continued to dance in the passenger seat.

I arrived in Dallas, Texas, on Wednesday and met up with Sam at the airport. She rented a car and we drove down to Ang's house in San Antonio. On our drive down Sam and I joked about our nervousness at the threat of a hurricane, but how glad we were that our flights did not get canceled and we were able to fly in today. We arrived at Ang's house and ran to the front door with glee. Ang was not concerned about the storm at all. "They worry about the storm all the time here," she said. "But the coast is so far away we're hardly affected. I'm sure it will rain this weekend, but that's about it. So let's make the most of these next two days before the rain hits on Saturday," she said.

My spirit felt light surrounded by friends. We enjoyed each other's company. First, we took advantage of the sunshine while it lasted and went tubing on a nearby river. We toasted to memories long gone and new ones yet to come with delicious wine. We visited wineries in and around Fredericksburg, Texas. We kicked the dust off our boots and tried our heels at line dancing at a local bar. We laughed. We cried. I was happy to connect with the feeling of smiling so hard my cheeks hurt.

I returned home with a full heart. I had one day to prepare for my interview. I decided to unpack, and then print copies of my resume and review interview questions. The next day I met Janet at the mental health agency. I proceeded to experience the longest interview I have had to date. We toured the Lighthouse, she asked questions, I answered. She introduced me to staff and two hours after I arrived, I departed.

. . .

Days passed as I waited for good news. Before I left the interview Janet warned me it may take some time because the non-profit organization verifies all the references I gave them. Patiently, I waited. I received contact from Janet, but it was about a delay; one reference had yet to be verified. I contacted the reference and let them know how to get in contact with Janet. A current of annoyance swept in. The temptation was like an undertow, strong enough to pull my mind away into worry. Luckily, my awareness muscle was strong after dedicated time spent in spiritual practice. I acknowledged the temptation, and I chose to keep faith. I did what I could to help the process along and then I chose to focus the rest of my energy on a new practice. Similar to what takes place in the practice of meditation, the mind wonders, and monkey mind arrives to play. When I notice that taking place, I connect to my breath with intention. I acknowledge where my thoughts went, and I choose to return to the present moment.

Five days into September, still no job offer. I recognized the outdated pattern to push to find a job and continue to apply to open health coach positions and chose something new. I chose to listen to the stillness in my gut that reverberated, *You got the job.* Instead of applying for different jobs online, I found my fingers reaching for *Moonology*, by Yasmin Boland. I flipped through the soft pages and landed on directions to a full moon ritual.

My curiosity led me to lay the reference aside and instead, play with what I thought a full moon ritual should be. I picked up my journal and wrote. I wrote about the old patterns that surfaced and what the temptation felt like to return to the familiarity of rushing around, working in customer service, scattering my energy, and playing it small. Tears streamed down my cheeks. *Breathe,* I told myself. Then, I switched to letting go. I wrote about letting go of the temptation to return to what once was. A temptation to hold so tightly to expectation–expectation to be fulfilled, and failure of the actions I took thus far to achieve that feeling of fulfillment.

I set my pen down and lit a candle. I found a guided full moon meditation and pushed play. The meditation ended, I picked up my pen and paper and wrote what I was grateful for in my life. I felt lighter like I could breathe easier. I felt the urge to move my body after sitting for nearly an hour. I decided to move in a way that not only benefited me physically, but that nurtured my mind and soul. I found a solar plexus yoga practice and rolled out my yoga mat.

Wednesday, the following week my phone rang and I felt myself catch my breath. "Hello," I answered. "Hello Kaitlyn, it's Janet calling about the Wellness Coach position. I'm pleased to invite you to be a member of our team." I smiled and let go of my breath.

When I hung up the phone I smiled big and did a little jig. Happy Dance! "I got the job!"

It pays to give into joy, I thought. #joywitch

About the Author

KAITLYN ALGAR

Kaitlyn, Psychic Moon Mentor, leads you to achieve the calm confidence needed to make money doing what you love. Kaitlyn guides you to connect with peace by walking with you through the darkness to embrace the deepest darkest parts of yourself. The Moon can teach you about your own cycles of emotions, thought, and behavior. Once you're aware of your cycles you're empowered to know how to work through them.

Kaitlyn began her career as a personal trainer and fitness instructor, later developing a holistic health coaching practice. After her own Spiritual Awakening in 2017, and a job loss she decided to incorporate spiritual practices into a mentorship program. Now, she teaches individuals how to trust their intuition and achieve peace in order to manifest abundance in their life and business.

Find Kaitlyn here:

https://linktr.ee/psychicmoonmentor

NINE

Sandra Joy

LETTING GO TO LEVEL UP: HOW TO CONQUER
COMFORT, FEAR, AND AVOIDANCE TO LIVE A LIFE
YOU LOVE.

Looking around at the contents of her life set up in neat little piles across the lawn, Christiana felt gutted, frightened, excited, and full of hope all at once. She was looking straight into the unknown and had been preparing for this moment for the past six months. The auction of her dream home where she spent the past decade was about to begin. Dreams change. She understood this all too well as she rode the waves of the past ten years. She wondered what life would bring her now. Ever prepared, she had a plan for her future alongside her husband and children. She was excited for new beginnings and the excitement that they always bring. Change has been the only constant in her life and she used to be hard on herself when things didn't work out as she planned. When she and her husband bought the small farmette a decade ago her dreams were full of everything she would create there. It would be her version of paradise with gardens overflowing with flowers and vegetables, horses grazing in the sunlight, and long, lazy, summer nights laying outside stargazing. She smiled as she remembered the old adage from Robert Burns about best-laid plans going astray.

· · ·

The auctioneer called out the first box lot and bidding began on the contents of her life: Items from her childhood home that traveled with her from place to place, brand new things that she never even had the chance to use but certainly the intentions. Bidders carried boxes away for 50 cents or one dollar, full of what was much more valuable to her than to them. Yet, with each fall of the gavel, she felt a weight lifted. It was as if she was shedding old skin and making room for a new, refreshed version of herself.

She needed to remind herself that holding on too tightly meant she wasn't moving forward. She was raised by depression-era parents who held on tightly to everything. She was admonished when she didn't put as much value into her possessions as her family had. She used to value her possessions as she was taught, then a moment arrived that shifted her perspective. She knew she was never going to move forward, never going to step into the new dream she had for herself if she continued to hold on to things from her past. She was tired of being stuck and wanted better opportunities for herself and her family. There was no rule that stuff had to stay with her forever. "My life is on the lawn," she thought as she gazed at everything that she had accumulated over the years, wondering how it managed to pile up.

It wasn't easy to let go of things. In fact, she used to hold on tight to everything because the more stuff she had the safer she felt. It was familiar, a reminder of where she had been and a constant fixture as she stepped into an unknown future. Except, this time, it was completely different. She was releasing the hold that possessions had on her and the guilt that caused her to carry them with her for so long. She earned those things: they had meaning and emotion for her. In fact, they weren't just things, they had become a definition of her place in the world. They were looks of approval from friends, status symbols, pieces of the trophy that was the life she chose to create. She realized this while gazing at the stars as she so often did.

The stars were there all the time and she didn't have to move them, pay for storage or transportation, wait for a sale, or use a coupon. She had arrived at the realization that things only have the power she gave to them and it was time to release the attachments that tethered her to a reality that was no longer for her.

In the months prior to the sale, she sorted through the years of possessions that she so readily accumulated and she realized that the act of purging was not just about getting rid of physical things, but it was also about letting go of emotional baggage. She had been holding onto things that no longer served her and actually held her back from her new dreams.

Christiana realized that by releasing her personal property, and the emotions and old ideals attached to it, it opened space for her to receive higher vibrational energy. This new, high-level energy that was created by releasing the old was beyond profound. She felt a sense of peace and clarity that she never experienced before. She was becoming aligned with a truer version of herself and living a more authentic existence. She couldn't help but feel grateful for the journey she had been on. Learning to purge people, places, and things that no longer served her was the key to her newfound happiness. She felt empowered by the act of letting go and making space for the new version of herself that was waiting right there for her when she was ready to embrace it.

Holding On and Letting Go

Have you ever held onto something for so long that it became a part of you? Something that you couldn't imagine ever letting go of, even if it no longer served you? We become so comfortable in our surroundings that any semblance of change can be a very difficult thing to manage. The reality is that everything carries energy and the more you surround yourself with it the more energy you are intentionally (or unintentionally) embracing. If you're feeling bogged down by the energy of something that no longer has a place in your life, know that it's okay to let go. The new energy and alignment you'll gain from releasing the old will outweigh the cost of carrying it with you.

Imagine your life is a basket. Every unnecessary thing you hold onto is like a rock in your basket, slowing you and weighing you down. These "rocks" also hold energy that can be heavy and cumbersome keeping you stuck. But if you let go of those heavy rocks, you create space for new and exciting things to come into your life. Holding on to them leaves no room for new and better to arrive, no matter how safe they make you feel.

We are held back in our comfort zones by self-limiting beliefs or by false or negative core beliefs. It can be extremely difficult to shed those negative core beliefs. So what happens? You define your life by those self-limiting and negative core beliefs. When in actuality, they are false beliefs that are doing nothing but keeping you from your best self and your greatness.

Change is like that. Fear is a natural part of it. You can stay where it's comfortable or you can step outside of that comfort zone and take a step toward yourself. Comfort and fear can be the same. Laying on the couch is not scary, it's comfortable, but staying in that emotional state of ease is actually suffocating your true potential. Being in the middle, in comfort, keeps us stagnant and tethers us to mediocrity. Do you really want to be mediocre? Are you really just average? I know you're not. I know you have so much potential and magic within you that is just waiting for you to get off the couch.

. . .

Stepping out of our comfort zones and into fear is not easy because we have been trained to stay on the couch. We have been taught to look for the quick fix, the latest pill that will ease symptoms and allow us to continue living a busy stressful hectic life, but we never look at the root cause to correct it - we just mask it. Our bodies are powerful powerful things and they listen to our mind. And if we hold onto stress and we don't have a good way of releasing it, it will show up physically in our body in some way. Consider the word disease: broken down, it becomes dis-ease. When we are not at ease with something and it causes stressors that we hold on to, those stressors start manifesting in physical ways. We literally make ourselves sick.

When we experience things that really upset us, that really fires us up we call those triggers. We attach those triggers to something that we believe about ourselves and it's usually something negative. So, instead of getting upset at the trigger itself, let's take a deeper look and analyze that trigger and figure out why we're reacting the way we are.

For example, we can often become triggered (and trigger others) by unwritten rules and expectations for our behavior. Women especially are not always given the respect that is deserved. Assumptions are made about our level of intellect (mansplaining), speaking out of turn, and unequal pay for the same work (Engineer vs. Woman Engineer). The triggers that action can cause when we break these unwritten rules may be daunting if we give them permission to be. Speaking your mind and standing up for yourself may bring nega-tive reactions from others and your personal reaction may be avoid-ance and shrinking back down to the status quo instead of standing in your power. You retreat to your comfort zone. But why?

.   .   .

Are you worried that people are going to track your every move? Spy on you? Judge you? Of course, they are! 100% in fact. So what? This is your chance to be unapologetically yourself and if people want to look and stare and point and criticize let them because it is a reflection of their insecurities that they're being so judgemental of you. Nothing should prevent you from living your life. When you spend all of your time putting your energy into what other people are thinking about you're stealing time from yourself that you could be using to be incredibly amazing.

You are not powerless. You have the innate ability to change any situation you find yourself in. At times, it may seem like a never-ending battle because so many obstacles fall into your path. It's times like those where giving up or just dealing with it or accepting it as a part of your life is going to be easier. It may feel easier but it definitely is not helping you. Thoughts like that come from fear and keep us stagnant. We cannot move forward, we cannot change, we cannot embrace new things if we constantly let ourselves live in the shadows of fear. Familiarity equals safety so that means the things that you're accustomed to and comfortable with give you a sense of security and a comfort zone. This is why people get stuck on the couch.

This is another place to pay attention to your emotions as well as the emotions of anyone close to you who may be directly affected by your decisions. The longer you stay in a situation that is no longer for you, the bigger the signs become. The signs will be fear-based because you are taking a step off of your comfortable couch. I know you've heard it before, but greatness and bliss are truly on the other side of fear. So, how do you know you are ready to step out?

It could be a new thought or an unexpected idea that really makes you excited. Have you had one of those yet? How have you talked yourself out of it? That's another thing that fear makes us do. Some people are experts at staying stuck because they have an excuse for everything simply because they do not have an answer for it. There's the secret my friends, not having an answer IS the answer. Sometimes you just need to trust and jump feet first knowing that your best and highest good is always at the forefront of your being. You will always be supported if you listen to the messages that you are given. You will always be greeted by a new door opening if you just listen and trust your instincts and walk through the fear.

Sometimes fear shows up in ways that you may not be ready for. Irritability, anger, prolonged silence, lashing out at others, even dependence on alcohol or other self-numbing substances. Fear can show up physically, mentally, and emotionally. Here's the secret to conquering fear when it arrives. Just know that fear is a safeguard put in place by your primal brain to keep you safe back in a time when fitting in meant staying alive. Today, you can create the opportunities you need to thrive, even if it means walking away from the familiar into the unknown. To be clear, fear is not without pain and sadness. I sobbed when I left my classroom after a 20-year teaching career for the last time. I had to say goodbye to a huge part of my life. It defined me for two decades. I was not only walking away from my classroom, I was walking away from every minute it took to earn two master's degrees in education, countless hours invested in lesson plans, and especially the friendships cultivated over the years. My choice was not the norm for the profession and I felt the judgment. It was judgment for not staying the course, not wearing the scars of the profession through to the end. And yes, ego has popped up a few times tapping me on the shoulder asking if I really made the right decision. And the answer is always yes. 100 times yes! Why? Because I chose myself.

Another lesson is avoidance. You can't avoid things, you have to face them, you have to analyze them and then you have to grow through them. It requires willpower and yes, you do have it. We are here to face our past, our choices, or anything that could be possibly difficult for us. You can't avoid it, you can only grow through it, and avoiding it is not going to propel you forward. We all have triggers that keep us in a place of lack. Whether they are people, things, self-limiting beliefs, stories we tell ourselves, or rooms we have created through experience and keep ourselves trapped inside. They exist to hold us back. It is our job to acknowledge them, work through them and let them go so we can embrace the parts of ourselves that are meant to shine.

A good place to start taking inventory of what is keeping you stuck is to think about your "Why" that brought the item, person, or experience into your life. Was it a coping mechanism? Was it there to fill a void? Was it a memory of a happy occasion? Was it used to fit in or impress others? Do you need it to be those things anymore? Tuning in to why it was there in the first place can help you release its hold on you. Be kind to yourself; it's okay to have a different opinion now than you did then.

Another way to help sort through what is holding you back is to look at the emotions you have attached to it. Is the item the true energy of the memory or is the memory itself the important part? Is it weighing you down with sadness? Does having this item make the memory more important, more valuable? What is happening to the space these items occupy? How is the energy in the space changing because of these items? What is the price you are paying by staying in the same, stagnant, stuck energy?

Another thing we tend to hold on to is other people's expectations. Living life to someone else's expectations can cause a lot of unnecessary emotional baggage. Guilt is a common feeling when you want to follow your own path but feel that you will let others down if you do. People also have an uncanny ability to guilt trip you for stepping outside of their expectations. When I retired from teaching two weeks before the start of a new school year, I was mostly met with support from my colleagues who knew why I was retiring. Yet there was one teacher who just laid on a thick guilt trip and said, "How could you do this to the students and parents?" I felt myself become immediately defensive and start to backpedal. Then I stopped. I looked at that teacher in the eyes and said, "That's where you have it wrong. I didn't do this TO the students and parents. I did it FOR myself." I knew what my soul needed and I listened. I put myself first knowing and trusting that everyone would be provided for, and they were.

It was not easy for me to walk away from a 20-year teaching career and the emotions and expectations of others weighed heavily on me. However, I stayed true to myself and my soul despite the intense fear that I felt and that made all the difference. When you follow your true path, doors open up for you and it turns out better than you could have imagined. You just need to trust yourself and allow yourself to release what is holding you back.

It wasn't until I learned how to purge people, places, and things from my life that I truly began to thrive. Learning to let go of something that had become a part of me wasn't easy at first. As I began to release the old patterns, I felt a new and higher level of energy coursing through me. It wasn't just about getting rid of physical belongings but rather about learning to grieve the loss of personal relationships and old ideals. It was about making peace with these losses at a soul level so that I could achieve a higher vibrational energy and a much more aligned existence.

Now, I look back on my life and wonder why I held onto things, people, and places for so long. I know it was necessary for me to learn those lessons and release what no longer served me, allowing me to grow and expand into the life I have now. The more I tuned in to my intuition, listened to my soul, and acted on those nudges the more success, peace, and love have shown up in my life. I no longer allow negative energy in my life. It exists and sometimes it tries to infiltrate my world in the form of people, situations, and fear. I recognize it now and send it on its way. I have no space for it or what it brings any longer.

Maybe it's not clear to you yet. You feel that something needs to change and you're not sure what it is. You feel it but you don't know how to define it. This is completely normal and the more that you listen to your heart, the more your path will be revealed to you. You have always known what you are meant to do. It may have become covered up by the expectations of others over the years. Maybe your path wasn't acceptable in your circle and you chose to do something that would garner approval instead. That's okay. We've all taken the easy (or not-so-easy) way out. The more that you listen to your heart the more you will know what is holding you back because it just doesn't feel aligned anymore. Look for patterns that shift or change completely for you. Something that once may have brought you joy now creates stress. If you can't put your finger on it, tune in to your body and feel your reaction to it.

Tuning in to Your Personal Energy

A good place to begin is to take a self-inventory of your energy. Where is it, where does it feel heavy or stuck? Are you holding onto old relationships, outdated beliefs, or things that don't serve you anymore? If so, it's time to purge. I know it might not be easy for you to let go but you will feel lighter and more energized as you do. It's not just physical things that need to be released; it's also relationships that drain your energy and beliefs that are not really yours.

. . .

When you do this, you will start to notice positive changes in your life, like meeting new people who share your interests and feeling more inspired than you have in a long time. You will also notice that you have more time and energy for the things that matter most to you. The new higher-level energy you have created by releasing your old patterns and making peace with those losses at a soul level is necessary to achieve higher vibrational energy. Holding onto things that no longer serve you prevents you from living your best life. However, letting go of those things comes with a level of fear of the unknown and that is completely normal.

A really good gauge of doing something that you are happy with is your level of energy when you're done. If you're doing something you're passionate about it's kind of like you're on a high after doing the thing you're great at. On the other hand, if you're doing something that doesn't agree with you and you are struggling to get through and it leaves you exhausted, wiped out, and empty, then you are doing something that is not for your highest good. These are some pretty powerful signals from the universe telling you what you should and shouldn't be doing. Yet we continue to let other people push us in directions that drain us. When it comes to following your soul's purpose and really reaching that piece of you that completely empowers yourself, you can't just talk about it. You actually have to do it. Take the steps. Make the plan. Move it forward. Release what is weighing you down. Your best life is truly waiting for you just on the other side of fear. It's time to get off the couch.

Begin to weave and the divine will provide the thread. ~Ancient Proverb

About the Author

SANDRA JOY

Sandra Joy is the founder and CEO of Healing Realms, LLC and Sandra Joy, LLC. She embraces the new energy consciousness of Earth and guides others to embrace this energy to connect and thrive in their soul purpose.

She is an Adult Indigo with a deep connection to Indigo, Crystal, and Diamond Children as well as a highly intuitive clairsentient. She is a Lightworker certified with Hands of Light, a Master Usui Reiki Practitioner, a Crystal and Color Energies Expert, a certified Hypnotherapist, a certified Oracle Card reader, and a 20-year activator of Indigo and Crystal Children.

Her purpose in this lifetime is to connect with people who want to learn how to harness the power of their energy system and thrive in their soul's purpose. She lives in Pennsylvania on a small farm with her husband, son, daughter, and many animals.

Find Sandra here:

https://linktr.ee/sandrajoylaratonda

TEN

Michelle Hamady

MAGICAL PORTALS DO EXIST

DISCOVERING THE MAGIC PORTAL

When I was young, I found mirrors fascinating. I would climb to the top of my dresser, pulling out drawers to use as steps and once there, I would just sit and stare. But I wasn't interested in my reflection, nor was I interested in the mirror image of my room. My gaze would take me to the space beyond where I currently was. It was like magic! The mirror appeared to create extra space beyond the wall and my five-year-old self wanted so badly to be in THAT space.

My life's journey would eventually lead me to discover a real-life magical portal. In 2010, I decided to pursue my master's degree in Transpersonal Studies. This curriculum not only provided opportunities to learn more about myself as an individual but to also explore the connection to the world around me as well as the consciousness beyond that connects us all. My heart was lit up by this! Since I always felt out of place in this world, this coursework sounded like a perfect solution. My hope was to finally find the answers to so many of my unanswered questions. Within this program, *Transformative Visual Arts* was the track I chose to specialize in. My desire was to feel more free in my creative self-expression again.

During the coursework, I creatively explored various forms of art. Each technique would reflect something meaningful and important back to me, but it was the mandala that literally opened up a whole new world to me - this was the portal I stepped through!

My first time exploring mandalas brought me face to face with my own reflection, a reflection I avoided, one I couldn't see clearly. My true essence was hidden and buried beneath the beliefs that distorted my self-perception.

The word Mandala is a *Sanskrit* term which loosely translates to "container of essence" and through this container of essence, I discovered a divine mirror that revealed the truth of who I am. My true essence was hidden and buried beneath the beliefs that distorted my self-perception. With each mandala I created, the process would safely transport me to moments of my past where I could retrieve a long-lost part of myself, heal my wounds, and bring more joy into the present by experiencing the magic and awe of the creation process.

As a child, I loved to create and draw. It didn't matter if it was clay, play-doh, or crayons while indoors or creating dirt caves and drawing with sticks in the sand while outdoors. There was freedom to create without worrying about what looked right or how it might turn out. That's the type of creativity we're all tuned into as children.

. . .

I remember in first grade, it was Christmas time and my classmates found out I drew reindeer. Of course, they all wanted me to draw one for them, too. Although they were excited and loved what I drew, I was so shy that the extra attention was uncomfortable.

Later that spring, there was an art contest that I entered. I remember my dad helping me create my art piece. It was so much fun gluing all the little toothpicks in place to form a picket fence and adding colorful ribbons cut to create the walls of the house. I ended up winning 1st place! The grand prize was $5.00 and back then, that was a lot of money for a little five-year-old! When I won, my dad proudly placed me on top of his shoulders and walked around with me sitting up so high, I felt on top of the world as he paraded me around!!

But I hid my art, just like I hid myself. When did this begin?

LOOKING FOR A PLACE TO BELONG

I was the oldest of three children and had a natural curiosity. I wanted the freedom to explore and experience and questioned everything that didn't make sense. And in my childhood, there was A LOT that didn't make sense. As a bi-racial child, I always felt out of place and because I was also extra sensitive, the world was really confusing to navigate. I longed for stability and a sense of safety.

Any opportunity to be outside surrounded by nature gave me that sense of safety I craved. It was pure freedom. Oh, how I loved to be barefoot in the grass! Even today, the memories of running through the backyard and doing endless cartwheels bring up so much joy. Just across the street, the woods were filled with paths and many hidden trails to explore. There was a lake at the end of the street where I would spend every day possible seeking out the different types of fish, tadpoles, turtles, and snakes. It felt so peaceful to take in the stillness of the water. Other times, it was exciting to investigate the splashes and ripples.

I loved New Jersey in the fall when the air is crisp and cool, and there's nothing like the smell of the woods, feeling the peace in the air. Nothing beats the colorful foliage of the north and I still remember the sound of the leaves crunching beneath my feet.

CONDITIONAL LOVE

Having a Korean mom, I experienced additional strict cultural beliefs. I was conditioned to believe I had to earn love, that my worthiness and value were based on appearances - don't bring shame to the family, be a good girl, be the obedient daughter, get good grades, etc. Staying on the honor roll in school was the only way to earn her acceptance and approval, and this kept me safe and on her good side.

My mom was far from being the patient, nurturing type. It seemed like she was constantly agitated and frustrated and I only made it worse. Have you ever heard the saying, "Stop crying or I'll give you something to cry about!"? We heard that one quite often in our home. I remember fearfully struggling to avoid water going into my eyes whenever she washed my hair. She'd resort to shoving my head under the faucet water to stop my tears and shut me up. My pain was perceived as an inconvenience to my mom and any time I expressed fear towards something (especially dental visits), the embarrassment she experienced would make her even more angry at me, so I learned early on to hide these feelings from her. Better yet, I just stayed out of her sight. It was much safer that way.

I was definitely a "daddy's girl" and my dad loved to take me everywhere he could. I had a tendency to walk on my toes and I remember him taking the time to teach me how to walk properly, holding my hand and repeating "heel/toe, heel/toe" while demonstrating this for me. He nursed me through a life-threatening bout with pneumonia and he was also the one who took the time to teach me how to color and draw. I loved how free I felt when I was creating art, not a care in the world!

POWER CREATED PAIN AND BEING SEEN WAS DANGEROUS

My dad was a master sergeant in the Infantry Division of the U.S. Army and I loved when he would take me with him to the artillery range. On the military base, he was surrounded by guns and weapons, so I knew my dad was powerful and always felt protected and safe with him. But one day, he asked a fellow soldier to watch me for a moment as he had to run up into the army watchtower. While he was gone, this soldier molested me. On the way home, I told my dad about this and it was never discussed again. Soon after, my own dad began molesting me. I was so confused why a person I loved would do this to me.

His behavior began to go through a drastic change. He was no longer the gentle, loving dad I knew. There was an explosive side emerging. He even tried to kill my mom. As my dad held the knife to my mom's neck, all my younger sister and I could do was scream and cry for them to stop. This powerful human who once made me feel safe was now terrifying to be around.

Many seeds of negative subconscious beliefs were planted by the time I was five years old. I had to dim my light in order to feel safe. I'm so grateful to have been surrounded by so much nature. It's where I felt the safest; out in nature I never felt the need to hide and knew I could escape anything if I had to. I felt so free being away from the chaos and confusion of home life.

LOOKING FOR SAFETY IN THE SHADOWS

Staying indoors during the cold winter months was quite a challenge. I spent all my time in my bedroom, hidden away, reading as much as I could while I waited for the weather to warm up. Thank goodness for my encyclopedia set! I could get lost for hours reading as much as I could. If an article ended with "See also" then I would pull the next referenced volume to do just that! Those rabbit holes were endless and so fun to explore. However, having to put away the stack of volumes afterward was not so much fun, but it was worth it. I would also spend my time drawing and by this time, those reindeer had long been replaced by horses. Their beauty and power captivated me. But I always tucked away any art I created and eagerly awaited the return to the safety of the outdoors.

When I was nine years old, things took another dark turn. My dad unexpectedly passed away. He had been in the hospital for a few months but the details of why were kept a secret from us kids. A close family friend had also recently passed, the son of my mom's friend - he was like an older brother to me. After my dad's death, my mom slipped into a deep depression (unknown to me at the time), and the guy who moved in 6 months after my dad passed also tried to molest me. This guy would become our stepdad.

Surrounded by so much pain and confusion, unable to detach from the overwhelming emotions around me, I slipped into my own deep depression at the age of 10. I tried to cut my wrists and also tried to overdose on pills. I'd retreat into the darkness of my closet and wish more than anything that I'd dissolve into the pitch-black nothingness. Adding to this pain and confusion, a few months before my dad's death my mom had chopped off all my hair in a fit of rage. My waist-long hair was shortened down to an inch in length. For a couple years after that everyone mistakenly thought I was a boy. The tremendous amount of shame that resulted from her anger and my embarrassment was anchored down into every cell of my body for many years to come.

Looking back, I'm honestly not sure how I even made it through that period. After a few suicide attempts, I shifted into self-mutilation as my depression transmuted into anger.

I managed to tap into the courage of my heart and ran away from home at the age of 14.

FOLLOWING MY HEART

It was a cold dark April night in 1984 when I climbed out of my bedroom window toward my freedom. I remember the mixture of fear and courage, uncertainty and determination, anxiety, and relief. In the darkness, my boyfriend was waiting for me a few streets over and we rode off on his moped. The next morning, a cop arrived at his house (my mom knew where I went). He had orders to kick me out onto the street. A struggle ensued between my boyfriend and the cop. We managed to escape, hid out in the woods for a while, and eventually made our way to his friend's house.

The friend's stepmom agreed to let me stay there, but my mom found out where I was at. After a couple of court visits, she agreed to let me stay there until the school year ended (school was very important to both of us) and after school, I was to be taken to the juvenile center.

When the school year ended, the friend's stepmom reluctantly dropped me off at the detention center. In this facility, I was surrounded by juvenile criminals and immediately felt so uncomfortable and out of place. I was a nerdy honors student whose only crime was running away from home.

Before I said goodbye to this amazing woman who had opened her heart and home to me, I was able to give her the name of an uncle who lived in Virginia. Luckily, she was able to track him down through directory assistance (there was no Google in the 80s) and he was able to make it to the next court date where the courts granted him custody.

SURVIVAL MODE AND WEARING THE MASCULINE MASK OF SUCCESS

Not one to be held back for long, I graduated high school a year early. I went from living with my uncle and his family to moving in with another aunt, obtained my first job, and completed my freshman year at a local university. As soon as I turned 18 I moved out of my aunt's home, excited for freedom again - so excited that I failed my sophomore year of studies. Over the years, survival mode remained strong and activated. But I was determined and resilient. Failure was never an option. I appeared successful on the outside, achieving anything I set my mind to. I thrived on external achievements, seeking external validation, but deep down I lacked self-worth and had no sense of self.

When I stepped into the corporate world, I thought I finally attained the security I was looking for. I got comfortable, and turned off the survival mode, but then became too comfortable. I lost all sense of self as I had no external milestones to accomplish that would further define my identity. It was time to drop all the masks, follow my heart and rediscover who I was. This is when I decided to pursue my master's degree in Transpersonal Studies. My mind argued and tried to push towards an MBA, that's what I'm *supposed* to do, right? But my heart just wasn't into that. It was time to follow my heart's intuition again, and I'm so glad I did!

As my master's program commenced, the coursework guided me through the process of unraveling and rebuilding myself from the inside out. This process brought about the profound realization of just how much, as an adult, I had completely lost touch with art and somewhere along the way I also lost the important connection with myself. Through many of life's events, I learned to hide my authentic self, to not stand out in any way, to not shine. Essentially, I learned to be chameleon-like in order to safely fit in among the crowd. I believed taking the chance of feeling any perceived discomfort from my self-expression was just not worth the risk.

My creativity was deeply buried under much fear and insecurities and my desire to rediscover and reconnect to it had been reignited. Through the visual arts courses, I began gathering up all the pieces/fragments left behind in order to reclaim them - self-love, identity, worth, value, creative feminine power. The mandala became the creative tool that allowed me to bring them through: together in wholeness, without constraint, without bounds, in a free-form expression. That's where the healing/alchemy begins.

ONE MORE TRY

Over the years, I tried to rebuild a relationship with my mom through phone calls and visits, but it always ended up with me in tears, feeling crushed. To make matters worse, I'd beat myself up afterward, replaying the scenes over and over in my mind, thinking I must have done something wrong. I must not have tried hard enough, right? The little girl inside was still hoping she could make it right.

Despite these challenges, I continued to work on learning how to love myself. Up to this point, my corporate job had provided me with years of stability. I was also fortunate to have a stable marriage during this time so I was able to focus on doing the necessary deep dive to face my most painful wounds. After an incredible amount of inner work and healing, I felt strong enough to deal with my mom again. The mother wound was the remaining area I was still longing for some healing in and now I was ready for one more try...

With my heart wide open and full of hope, I called my mom. I can't remember how the call started but I remember the moment when my mom decided to ask if the abuse that happened with my dad was true. For a moment, I felt my little girl light up. She was so excited to finally have the healing she had always wanted! After all these years, this was finally going to be addressed and brought out to the open.

. . .

"Yes, it's true," I responded.

My mom then asked, "Why didn't you tell me when it happened?"

As I began to explain, the words came out of my mouth, "He told me not to…" I had flashbacks to how powerful my dad was, and how I never dared to disobey him.

Before I could continue, she blasted me through the phone, "How dare you tell anyone about this! You should have kept your mouth shut! I've had to live with this shame and embarrassment all these years because of YOU!!"

My little girl was blindsided. The last words I heard before my mom hung up on me was to not even show up at her funeral. I was absolutely stunned.

Here I was at the age of 48, crushed again. Adding to that I felt like an orphan, completely abandoned. The little girl inside of me died at that moment. The dream of having a mother's love and acceptance just ended, and now I felt so lost.

As I grieved through this process, I realized it was now up to me: to be the inner mother to my inner child. I took my inner child by the hand, it was up to me to love and accept her and help her through this. She was not alone, she was not abandoned.

After I'd had some time to process my pain, I realized I was just given a gift. I was now free - completely free. I could drop all the expectations, the failures, and the shame I'd been carrying. It was time to be free to express myself, live from my desires, and completely accept myself for who I am. All the love and acceptance I had been seeking had been within me all along.

Several years later, I received an unexpected message that my mom had sold the childhood home I had known. The home that has been energetically a part of my life for almost 50 years. I pulled up the sales listing online. The house was a box of memories. Some of those memories sprinkled throughout my childhood are those I will always cherish as they bring a smile to my face and joy in my heart. Others are more deeply embedded and I am grateful for the wisdom they now reveal.

As I click through the home's exterior photos taken under a clear bright blue sky, I see the image of my bedroom window. It's such a stark contrast from that cold dark April night when I climbed out to my freedom. I'm so grateful that the 14-year-old Michelle used that window as a portal and bravely stepped through to begin to create life on her terms.

I'm reminded that with love and courage, anything is possible. It takes courage to reunite with the heart and embrace the freedom to express what may have been hidden dormant for many years, possibly many lifetimes.

REFLECTIONS THROUGH THE HEART

Through reconnecting with art, I was able to transform feelings and perceptions of unworthiness and not belonging. Releasing layers of conditioned beliefs that were not mine to carry any longer meant more of my authentic self could shine through as I reclaimed those fragments that were long lost and/or buried. The things that once made me feel different and out of place became the qualities I've learned to appreciate as I embrace my uniqueness. I was afraid of the light and found comfort in the darkness, embarrassed to be me, believing it dangerous to be seen.

The mandala reflected back not what I wanted to see but what I needed to see. It placed me at the edges and gave me the courage to step beyond. As I began to view myself through the lens of my soul and not through the eyes of my broken human, self-love and acceptance allowed me to see my own beauty and uniqueness.

Experiencing the healing power of art was a crucial piece of the puzzle to the story of my transformative journey as I healed from the inside out. I realized I couldn't see the beauty in my art because I could never see the beauty in myself. I've spent my life seeing and judging myself through the critical harsh eyes of my mom and the unconscious messaging I received from her. I always felt ashamed of who I was: never enough, unlovable, and unworthy.

Because I followed my heart and intuition, my soul was able to lead me back to myself to rediscover the truth of who I am. The parents my soul chose to have in this lifetime provided the perfect challenges and obstacles for me to break free, recognize my strengths, and claim my full potential.

When I look into the mirror now, I see myself clearly. I'm not looking in the mirror to escape or hide or run away. I see the beauty and my essence reflected back to me.

. . .

I embrace the wholeness of who I am. I'm grateful for the gifts I've collected over the years.

I invite you to take a look at your soul's journey through a different lens, no matter how hard or difficult you might think that is.

Are you willing to see how each event or situation becomes an adventure in this kaleidoscope of life? When viewed through the eyes of our soul, the broken pieces we see are the necessary fragments that magically come together to form a beautiful unique mosaic.

You are born worthy, you are born precious. You are the gold.

It's my honor to help guide others in remembering who they are so they, too, can create more magic, joy, and freedom in their lives.

We are the creators and the creation. The journey through life brings us back to ourselves. Through this process, we keep creating, re-creating, and discovering ourselves in every moment.

You are living your soul's alchemy.

About the Author

MICHELLE HAMADY

Michelle is a Creative Possibilities Alchemist and transformational coach. She is passionate about helping others experience their own power so that they remember their beauty, strength, and creative potential. She offers an innovative transformational process to guide individuals through their own self-discovery and healing journey to reveal just how amazing they truly are.

As a lifelong learner fueled by curiosity, she has discovered that life's aha moments are abundant and the possibilities are endless in the self-development journey.

Michelle has traveled to many energetic vortexes such as the pyramids and temples of Egypt, Petra in Jordan, the Patagonia region in Chile, Morocco, Easter Island, the Canary Islands, and Sedona, AZ. Her spiritual journeys have instilled the courage necessary to navigate within a chaotic corporate world while remaining soul-centered. She has recently retired after 25 successful years within the corporate world, to focus her time helping others to experience their own heart expansion through creative expression.

She believes we're all here to make our unique contribution to the world. By healing one heart and soul at a time, each of us can make an impact that will be felt in the world around us.

Find Michelle here:

Website: https://michellehamady.com/

Facebook: https://www.facebook.com/michelle.hamady/

Linktree: https://linktr.ee/michellehamady

ELEVEN

Jessica Verrill

UNCHARTED TERRITORY

I don't want to die.

The thoughts circled around and around my head.

I'm not ready.

There is so much I haven't done.

So many places I haven't been.

So much love I haven't given.

I don't want my daughter to lose me. More than she already has.

. . .

My mission is not complete.

I'm not sure which of those last two statements stung the worst. And yet, when I really feel into it, there is an intertwining of them. Healing myself, raising consciousness, and giving my child the best foundation she can have is of utmost importance. After decades of personal development, learning, and practicing energetics, I understand the complexities of the human spirit and the impact that experiences can have on us for lifetimes. I choose consciousness as often as possible–I am still human after all–and strive to live that in my parenting, business, relationships, and life. And when I go off course or fall out of alignment, opportunities arise to bring me back to center–often in the form of a health crisis or dis-ease. Yes, I said opportunity: lessons, possibilities, and a re-emergence of self.

I am mindful to not let the challenge or a diagnosis define me. I am conscious of no longer saying, 'I have Lyme Disease.' So often in our culture, we allow these labels to define us, without even considering the costs or the impact it has on ourselves. We allow our situations, challenges, and perceived lack of abilities to define us and the life we live. We allow ourselves to succumb to the victim mentality and to fall into that darkness that distorts our reality, taking hold of every molecule of us, as we grasp onto any shred of hope we have left. It comes in deep, dark, like a storm cloud enveloping your entirety until you can see nothing else in or around you.

As we surrender to the lessons, the beauty within this cocoon of density, we begin to see the glimmer of light. Hope. Connection. Love. Not from somewhere outside of us, but deep within. And to truly access this center, we so often need a catalyst of a situation or experience to lure us into the deep. Even as spiritual beings, we are continually working with or looking to the light. What feels good? Where is the light? Yes, these are important things to consider, but so often this is in disregard to the depth of potential that is found only through transcending the weights on our soul that have been accumulated through lifetimes of ignorance, lessons, and pain both endured and inflicted.

Humans are interesting in that they are mentally programmed to look for the negative in situations however we tend to want to avoid pain at all costs—even or sometimes especially when we are in another form of pain. Comfortably uncomfortable. The comfort we know, even though it may be an extremely excruciating battle of discomfort that is endured daily, is the one we so often stay with because it is known, it is relatively safe (even when it isn't), and here's the big one: it's easier.

Humans seem to prefer discomfort over change. Despite their desire to achieve better outcomes or feeling unsatisfied with their current situation, people often choose to stick with familiar habits and patterns even if those habits and patterns cause pain or suffering. This is because change is perceived as challenging and requires effort, whereas staying in their comfort zone is seen as easy and effortless. Additionally, fear, uncertainty, lack of motivation, or fear of failure also contribute to a reluctance to change. Therefore, by choosing discomfort over change humans continue to experience the same problems, face the same obstacles, and fail to reach their full potential.

When we continue to lean into this uncomfortable certainty in our lives, we so often miss the flashing lights directing us from the current road we are on, leading us to a broken bridge and trouble, which can be manifested in so many ways. A big one being our health, but also the breakdown of partnerships, relationships, business challenges, and/or the development of passivism and melancholy in our lives. Everything begins to deteriorate until it reaches the boiling point of us not being able to push it aside. The perpetuation of unease or dis-ease in our lives presents us with yet another choice, perhaps the greatest one of all: Continue on and treat the symptoms or seek to find the lessons, silver lining, and messages all wrapped up within the apparent thorn in our lives.

How can we reconnect to ourselves after investing so much in carefully creating the masks and personas to fit perfectly into the societal expectation of ourselves? How can we move through the challenges not only with grace and balance but also with a deeper understanding and connection with our essence, our soul, and the meaning of it all?

We look to nature for signs. We look to oracle decks, tarot, crystals, the guru, seek the blueprints, listen to others on how they achieved perfect health, the 6 figure business, harmonious relationships, and a marriage that always feels like a honeymoon. We seek all of these things to find the truth, our truth, our path, receive clarity, guidance and answers. We want to know it all, like watching the highlight trailer of our lives. There will be heartache, challenges, and despair, but through perseverance, the star always comes out the star. Winning. Happy. Enlightened. I get the appeal and the seeming need for this. I have been here, more times than I can count. Our whole lives we are typically taught that others know better than us. We are conditioned to be followers, to be worker bees, to produce, and to seek the what, why, and how from some other authority.

But how often do we remember to look within *ourselves*? The disconnection from our truth, our wisdom, and our guidance has become so prevalent, even within the spiritual communities. It is often portrayed that there is some magic blueprint or training that will teach you everything you need to be happy, and have a successful career and relationship. But is there?

. . .

Of course, you can find support outside of you. You can seek insight through all of these things and they can be immensely helpful, especially when we aren't aware of our own limitations and perceptions. The challenge is not in the tools but dependence on the tools to dictate our lives. Many go from a parent who knows better, to the school teacher that knows better, to the guru who knows better. See a pattern here? The imbalance is in the dependence on these tools and support.

I truly believe that a big portion of this is from the desire, need, and deep aching to feel special. As we are navigating our way through life and spirituality, someone tells us that we are here for big things, that we are from a lineage of–insert current accolades in the spiritual world–then we receive the deep acknowledgment and affirmation that we are special. Everything is going to be okay and we are going to have the ending of that feature movie we are starring in. So, we continually give our power away, over and over, to others that promise to help us access that specialness within. Now, you don't need me or anyone else to tell you that you are special, here on a special mission, or have immense power within you. Do you have a soul? Well, then the answer to all of those is yes. And this won't look the same for anyone. We need people with magnificent ability, connection, compassion, and ability in ALL spheres of life–if it is truly fulfilling and aligned with *you*. Not me, not your favorite guru, not the amethyst sphere on your desk, not your partner or best friend. *You*. What works for me, most certainly will not work for you, not in all components anyways.

Therein comes the challenge. How do we know what is aligned with us? How can we access this power and infinite guidance within?

. . .

Only with consciousness and the ability to see how and where we are giving our power and authority away to others, we are able to begin to dismantle it. We begin to grant greater access to internal power by untangling everything that has prevented us from doing so before—most of all ourselves. As we take radical responsibility for the actions we have and haven't taken, we uncover our voice and allow it to be used. We uncover our soul's truth and we become increasingly able to discern what is and is not for us.

Imagine a lush landscape full of vines, trees, and brush. Somewhere within this forest, there is the treasure, the gold, the item that is sought by many far and wide. The landscape creates a sometimes treacherous journey to it, one that reveals many insights and beauty along the way. As we move through these layers of conditioning, personal limitations, and beliefs, we move closer to our goal. For decades movies portray these same stories in many ways and while we see it as a physical hunt and exploration, throughout the voyage those on this quest receive so much more internally. The stars of the show learn how to harness our strengths, how to overcome our limitations with courage and bravery, and how to persevere when all we want to do is give up and retreat, just as we have the opportunity to.

The journey of connecting with ourselves and our personal power is much the same. We succumb to enormous challenges that we feel may break us. We break through what we are told we should do, to what we know is true for ourselves, often alienating ourselves from relationships and our stable place within the status quo. Once we begin to excavate and gather these nuggets of gold within, while the thought of turning back may be tempting, elements of ourselves are returned and propels us forward when we are wary. The discomfort of change becomes a new level of comfort for a while as we believe and trust that the treasure of healing, alignment, and bliss is truly within.

. . .

However, eventually, even those on this journey of self-discovery and healing get tired, exhausted, lose their way, become over-ambitious and push too hard, or have neglected some element of the experience for the body, mind, emotions, or spirit. We ignore the cues that we took a wrong turn, that we need more rest, that our relationship is no longer aligned, that this partnership isn't in our best interest, the foods we are eating aren't nourishing us, or we don't recognize the damage the deeply held trauma and emotional cycles are causing and we push through for something that feels more important at the time. Once I get to this goal, this place, done with this project, I'll change my schedule. Once I eat this food, I'll buy healthier. Once I have more time, I'll address the imbalanced relationships.

Until you don't. Then your system decides that it needs to get your attention in a bigger way. If you aren't paying attention to the trail markers on the trees, then pretty soon a boulder will be in your way and that often comes as an illness or dis-ease manifest in your body, mind, finances, or all of the above. None of us are immune; as someone who has studied and practiced energetics, mindfulness and has a background in health & wellness, I still found myself here. I can look back and see exactly the choices I made that contributed to burnout, which weakened my systems to the point of caving to the underlying illness present: Lyme disease, Bartonella, Babesia, and a massive Epstein-Barr virus flareup.

Talk about knocking me down. The excitement I had about building my new publishing business had led me to fall into old patterns of overworking, pushing myself when I was tired, and hustling to make things happen. Even when I knew I couldn't keep up the pace, I continued to. One particular evening comes to mind. My family had gone to the mountains to an old lodge where we were staying to do some snowmobiling. Not my favorite, but my husband loves it and it is always a fun change of scenery. I had recently opened up a book project and had dozens of interested people messaging me, asking questions, and getting information while I determined if it was a good fit. I spent most of the evening on my phone outside of our room at the great stone fireplace that was lit in one of the common centers because it was the only place I could connect to WI-FI. Looking back I see the fears that were motivating me. The fear of missing out, of not immediately being available and not connecting with a potential client, and the fear of failing. This fear of failing motivated my actions so much that I dropped my boundaries and sacrificed what is most important to me: my family and my health.

Illness, with the loss of physical capacities and the emotional, mental, and spiritual strain that creeps into every single facet of your life stands to undermine every single thing you have created. We can look at it as a reckless persecutor admonishing us to a life of instability and pain through the havoc it creates. Or, we can look at the chaos and destruction as possibilities. When we are stripped away, beaten down, and challenged to operate as we once did, everything goes under a microscope. Is this important to me? Is this a priority? Is this worth my limited energetic output? Can this wait or does it have to be now? Everything and I mean *everything* is put under this lens. As you begin living in this way, it becomes so apparent that this is how it always should be. I went on so many weekly calls that were exhausting to me and quickly took them out of my schedule. Projects needed to be in full alignment. Events and outings were skipped or minimized.

I stopped reaching out to support or check in on others and in doing so, I noticed how much energy I was putting into helping friends, family, and acquaintances and how little of that I was receiving. So much of my life and relationships were off balance. I love helping people and giving support but found myself overgiving in so many aspects of my life. I mourned the relationships, I slipped a bit into victim mentality from time to time (what's a good life check without the deep lessons?), and I deeply longed for support, even at the fraction I had put into others. I changed my business policies and no longer gave my schedule link freely. I had so many people connecting with me, asking lots of questions, getting information, and then moving on. So, I had been doing LOTS of free consultation calls. I had to get real and get firm with myself. I was running a business after all and it was damn time I positioned myself as a business owner with a need to have income and to close gaps and leaks. I'm not Google and my time isn't limitless.

I am not in a place where I am able to overgive or have loose boundaries. At every turn, I am being asked to connect to myself and gauge the alignment of any given thing. I don't have the luxury of looking the other way, overstepping my needs, or pushing myself to exhaustion. Any of this could push me back in my healing and undermine everything I have worked so hard for.

And for all of it, I'm grateful for the lessons. The life check. The reassessment of priorities and understanding of myself and my goals. My life was off-track and I've had this opportunity to look at every element and consider if it is for my highest good and if that is truly what feels best. How powerful is this?

As I do so, I understand and profoundly value connecting to one's voice. The power. The truth. The guidance. I've known this of course, but every time we are invited, initiated, or pushed into this space of survival-meets-potency-meets-chaos, we have the choice to go further. To access deeper realms of possibility within us and to carry that torch forth. When we elevate our personal power, we raise the energetics of the collective, we offer a glimpse into the metamorphosis of potential for all. We break ancestral patterns and heal the DNA and the energetic bloodlines. We carve the path forward so that others who come after us–like my daughter–have the ability, courage, and inspiration to move our planet into uncharted territory, where I hope it is the norm to follow your truth, find your voice and strive for personal alignment, regardless of what that looks like.

So persevere. Trust. Lean in. More. Find your voice. Use it loudly. Be the catalyst. You are needed. You are loved. And yes, you are special.

About the Author

JESSICA VERRILL

Jessica Verrill is an energetic alchemist, intuitive channel, and USA Today Bestselling Author. As the founder of House of Indigo, a multimedia publishing company, she supports leaders in sharing their unique gifts and creating a product suite that packages their intellectual property into books, oracle decks, and companion workbooks.

As an intuitive and energetic alchemist, Jessica is a true visionary and utilizes this power with her clients through creative visioning and soul-aligned strategy. A life-long learner, she is often immersed in books and classes, including herbalism and flower essences, health, wellness and personal development, spirituality, and enhanced psychic development.

Jess lives in Maine with her husband, daughter, black lab, and cat. She loves gardening, communing with nature spirits, hiking, exploring nature, being around water, traveling, and personal development.

Find Jessica here:

https://linktr.ee/jessicaverrill

TWELVE

Len Blea

DEATH REBIRTH

When I was born, it was with the umbilical cord wrapped around my neck twice and I was blue in the face. They didn't know how long I had gone without oxygen or how many brain cells had passed. The doctor unwrapped the cord and immediately spanked me to try to get me to breathe. It took me many, many years to realize that even coming into this world I was fighting to arrive. That was my first near-death experience. That was the gateway to the death doula rebirth doula work that I do. My mother was told that there was a test that could be done to determine how many brain cells had died but it wasn't completed. Sometimes when I close my eyes, I can see myself as a baby being held by my feet and the cord being untangled while the doctor rubs my back, trying to get life into me from the cord.

This chapter is a series of true, unexplained experiences; they were not voluntary. Whether it was a divine presence that was with me, whether it would be called a vision or visitation, whether it be called a near-death experience, out-of-body experience, whether I was in an altered state or realm, they just happened. When we realize that there's more to this realm than what we can see with our physical eyes, unexplained things occur. They come when they need to and, when they are embraced and acknowledged, it opens doors to opportunities for unimaginable, unexplainable, and truly life-changing experiences.

When I was around the age of 12 or so I was going to change a light bulb. The lamp was plugged into the wall. I didn't think anything of it. I tried to remove the light bulb. I touched the metal part of the lamp and the light bulb at the same time. This caused the lamp to electrocute me. I felt the voltage of the electricity running through my body. It burned and it hurt so badly. My family yelled at me, "Len let go of the lamp, throw it down!" As I shook and moved across the floor I said, "I can't." My voice vibrated because the electricity was that deep and strong. I don't know where it exited out of my body, but I was so scared that it could have crossed my heart, I could have died. I could have been electrocuted to death. There was such pain from the electricity, such physical pain that ran through my body for what seemed like several minutes. It might have just been seconds but it felt like forever. I could feel it traveling through me. I couldn't feel any pain in my head but it was through my whole entire body. I could feel it in my arms, I could feel it in my chest, I could feel it in my legs. Finally, I just threw the lamp because the electricity exited my body. I don't know from where the electricity exited out of my body. To this day I still experience shocks, whether it's on my lips or hands from water, from walking a short distance, or when my caregiver shocks herself as she touches metal when pushing me in my wheelchair.

When I was about 27, I was living in an apartment on the second floor. I had this dream that there was a lightning storm and that I was in the shower during this lightning storm. Lightning struck the building and I could feel shocks on the bottom of my feet and they burned so badly. The shocks reminded me of the lamp and the pain that I felt from it. After that dream, for a year and a half later when there would be a lightning storm I could feel shocks in my fingertips and up and down my arm. Those same shocks I could feel in the shower. There was no coincidence that any of these things happened. They continued.

In 2010 I was heading to work and it was a snowy day. I merged onto the highway from the on-ramp. As soon as I merged onto the highway I hit ice and started spinning out of control. I was barely on the road but realized I needed to get off quickly and safely. As I steered off the side of the road I could feel a presence was holding up my 4Runner. I should have flipped but I didn't. Multiple cars pulled off the side of the road to make sure that I was okay. Considering the shock that I should have been in, my pulse never got above 80 that day, and my blood pressure was not high that day, as it had been in the past. I knew there were Angels holding me up so that I wouldn't flip. I had never felt so protected as I did at that moment. I'm grateful for the protection always. Grateful for knowing that there are higher beings and energies out there ensuring that I'm safe and knowing it's not time to go yet.

Many years ago my friends and I were in New Mexico picking pine sap from the pine trees as it was the glue that I used to use for my artwork. An artist friend at the time and I were picking from the same tree. I was picking from the bottom of the tree because there was no way that I could physically climb the tree. Meanwhile, George climbed the tree and screamed my name, "Len! Len!" His screams were long, drawn out. I didn't do anything because I thought maybe he's hit the mother load of sap and he was letting me know he hit a gold mine. I was excited. I heard a couple of branches snap. I didn't stand up. The next thing I knew George was falling, landed flat on my back, bounced off of my back, and landed next to me. My back bounced maybe two or three inches if even that. A branch that was next to me poked my side, but that was it. I wasn't knocked down or hurt. My back didn't hurt. I was more concerned about George than I was about me. George could not understand how he could not have hurt me at the rate he was falling and then hit me. Shortly after that, my friendship with George ended as he remained in disbelief that I wasn't hurt and he couldn't understand the reasoning behind the grace of the situation.

My sister passed away in 2011. I so intensely longed to go home. When my father passed in 2006 I had longed to go home as well. For me, all of my life I've felt that this is not home; this physical realm is a temporary home. My soul knows and feels a longing for a place that's not here. I've never been comfortable in the human body; this world is so dense. I know there's something more than this. Home to me is with the Creator, the Divine, Source, and the Universe.

In August 2011 I entered an altered state and my soul left my body. I was pulled over to the other side because all was white and there was a beautiful brown lion. He looked at me and I looked at him. It was blissful and relaxing. I had no fear. I didn't realize it at the time but I was on the other side. As I continued in this altered state, I was then playing Putt-Putt golf with my nephew; we were wrestling and I was getting muddy. I told my nephew sadly, "I have to go. I'm going to pick pine with my friend Gary in Walsenburg." I left, got into my red Toyota 4Runner and I started driving. Still in the altered state. It was an overcast cloudy day and as I started driving from Denver, I felt myself being pulled from the car kicking and screaming because I knew where I was going. I'm being pulled again through the clouds, still kicking and screaming. I'm pulled four times, resisting each time until I arrive on the other side. There is the lion again. It's white everywhere. Behind the lion, there is a lioness. I am then presented with an exit point and asked if am I going to take it. I declined.

There's so much that I need to do, that I need to teach, knowledge that I need to share and so much left to do. I believe it was God who had explained to me how many opportunities I had before this and how many exit opportunities were left. I understood the terms that were given to me and I came back. When I came back into this physical realm, I came into my body so hard that I literally jolted and came up about two inches off the bed.

That day in the physical living world, I was to go pick pine with Gary. That day was overcast, just like the sky was in the altered state I was in. I kept pointing to the sky telling myself, "Today is not the day, today is not the day!"

I became obsessed with wondering if each situation was another exit point, making it hard to fully live. I was so obsessed with my death that I wasn't really living. When I spoke to a hypnotherapist about it, she said "It's interesting how most people are going and it's not their time and they're being sent back but you're being pulled and you're saying I don't want to go." That was an interesting fact but it made so much sense because it's not time. I'm not claiming to play God. I'm not claiming to play that I can control when I'm going to go because it's not that. God and I know when it is going to be time. There will be no fear, there will be no worry, and there will be nothing but bliss and readiness.

As an adult, I got into the shower and there was a lightning storm outside but I needed to go to work, and that entailed showering first. I could hear the thunder and I knew it was risky because of the lightning and potential strike while showering. I was showering and suddenly heard a voice. It seemed like it was in my head; it said "Get out." I think I can't get out, I'm not done. I heard the voice again "Get out. Get out now." I don't get out, I lift my foot and I feel a shock. I remember feeling that shock and it didn't matter that I wasn't done showering, I got out. That shock from the shower reminded me of the dream, the electric shock from the lamp, and all of the other times that all the electricity ran through me.

In January of 2023, I had another experience that felt like a dream but was not a dream as I slipped into an altered state. I was with several people with Jesus leading the group. Jesus told us that in less than 24 hours we would all die. He told us to grab something for breakfast when we leave in the morning and that we should all sleep so that we would be rested for the day. In the morning I grabbed more than what was needed for breakfast and I was running behind. Everyone had managed to escape through a single black door quickly and quietly. This door was by itself in this brightly huge, glass-filled office but I was caught. All around me were people wanting to hurt me but all I needed to do was make it through this door. I was able to make it through the door and as soon as I did, there was Jesus in the middle of a field and also a lady and a man with guns. I kept walking forward with the rest of the people as everyone began falling from being shot. I remember being saturated with blood and knowing that it was from the bullet. Jesus then said "Rise all of you for you are not dead" and I Rose. Shortly after that, I came back to this reality. If that was not an exit point opportunity, I do not know what it was. I could feel the blood. I could feel falling. I couldn't feel pain because death doesn't hurt.

With each near-death experience, lessons and beauty came into my life. Especially the one in 2011 when I was pulled over. I don't think very many people have a choice like that because most people want to go. From then on I was quite concerned about not leaving before my time. But from that, I was also able to see life as it truly is. In an instant, we can go from this world to the next. It's not painful. It's just this beautiful transition that happens and we all go exactly when we need to. It's like a rebirth. The rebirth from this life to the next. Then when we return, we rebirth from that life into this. A continuous cycle of rebirth. Like the flowers, the seasons, the trees, the leaves, everything. These experiences can help us realize that life is really worth living. It can show us that we can go against the grain, we can live, and be who we truly are, not what society wants us to be. That's the beauty. It helps us to make peace with pain and suffering, knowing that we may never be healed completely but we can still live and be alive. Source, Divine, Creator, God, Goddess, all the light beings know that when it's our time, they come to embrace us. Death is not painful as people believe it is. If we always fear death and fear the unknown then can we truly live? For every day we die a little and every day we are reborn a little. It's all about perception.

When you are working with death so closely it can sometimes cross into your life, cloud, and confuse you with which world are you really living in. Although this happens, it brings us beauty about knowing that everything is always temporary, how beautiful death really is. That is, if we really, really look at the world, the flowers, the trees, and the seasons. What really is death? What is it but a rebirth? That is the beauty of being able to experience the between worlds.

This part of the chapter is a channeled message from source. Questions are asked, and messages are given.

Why is it that you must always seek what you fear?

Why can you not lay down and be put in the grass and know that it's just transformation?

. . .

The beauty of death is that it does not necessarily exist as all windows remain in the soul and shed the body. The body is just the vessel you've chosen in this existence, in this incarnation to wear. It doesn't necessarily define your soul but it enhances your experiences.

It allows you to feel the love between the existence of the non-existence. It allows you to exist in a form that is dense and it completes your cycle by learning what you need to learn being here for who you need to be here for and expressing what needs to be expressed.

Death is but a beauty.

Because when you can embrace when something is coming forward and you leave this existence of this world, you return to your true natural form. Everything is different but it's so beautiful.

To be a pure soul in its true essence is TO BE without weight of a body and to just be in the Bliss of love, essence, existence, purification and light. Not having to worry about breathing, clothes, taste, and uncontrolled feelings. Not worrying about the mundane that the flesh has to worry about.

Death brings about the freedom, the joy, the love, the life, and the consciousness.

. . .

Without consciousness we would not exist because we are part of the consciousness of the creator; we return to where we came from, to the Bliss, to the beauty, to the love, and to the Divine.

We return to the freedom that we so much seek in this physical form yet in this physical form there's so much that could be accomplished. It just needs to be looked up and addressed in such a way.

Can you explain death more in detail so that the souls in the flesh can understand?

There is light in the dark and dark in the light; there's always balance between the worlds.

It is not a physical death as we see rather a rebirth of the soul into the many incarnations that the soul arises to.

At times the souls travel in groups. At times the souls travel alone. At times the soul does not travel at all but rather stays and waits for the next incarnation as it gathers all of the information that is needed.

The suits, the house, the shell, whatever is referred to as what the soul wears is that it is a dense form yet the human mind can understand the density. It's an illusion but not.

When one transforms, one becomes and when one becomes, one transforms.

. . .

All is always intertwined.

We put labels and words to something and when we look for the right words, we forget the most important parts. The most important part of death is that of the experience, the feeling, the love, the freedom, not the letting go of the One world to the other, but the freedom of release of returning to the wholeness and the oneness that the self has.

It is remembering the Christ consciousness. It is remembering the all is, remembering the one is, remembering the I Am.

It is returning to Source and the love that has always been there that's never left.

What advice can you give people who have near-death experiences that struggle with not wanting to go before their time?

Death is not something fearful and upon death, everything that needed to be completed would have been completed.

The opportunity to pass away while having a near-death experience is about knowing that this is an opportunity to do so. It does not matter whether everything has been completed or not in the person's mind. The soul contract has been completed. This is something that the human mind cannot comprehend at times but the soul can.

. . .

Many believe that Ascension is the only way that one can leave this human form which is not the case. Completion of the soul contract is what is.

When one completes everything then one will return to Oneness. Upon returning to Oneness, there will be no concern of unfinished business as there will only be completion.

Time on the human level is so different from time in the spiritual world. It is non-existent in the spiritual world. It is something that is programmed into the human psyche. Time is programmed with numbers and definitions of them, yet how is it intuition and the soul know when. When the intuition and the soul can see that everything is aligning as it should be, then why should one question, *Am I going before my time?*

There is no need to; the soul just knows. Embrace that the soul knows the mind and the ego is trying to play the tricks of time.

Any last messages for everyone?

Near-death experiences should not be fearful.

When one experiences a near-death experience they see there is no body, there is no weight, there is no illness, there is nothing but bliss. With this opportunity, one returns to Oneness, and even though it is not their time to go, it should help one to relax and to see that when one's soul returns the beautiful Bliss is there.

. . .

We hope that near-death experiences help people to help others, and educate them that death is not a fearful place.

Death is that of beauty.

It's just one transition from one world to the other removing the shell, that human form that was once used to house a soul. We hope that one will look at death as a rebirth, as a beauty as something that is not painful.

We wish you well and we will be there in the times of need and we will welcome you home with open arms, bliss, love, light, and all the wonderfulness that the soul returns to.

As the channeled messages close, I would like to give thanks to the Divine, Source, God, Goddess, the Universe, and all who helped with the Divine channel to messages that were provided in this chapter. I would like to say thank you for the messages. I would like to say thank you for allowing me to be the channel ensuring these messages on their behalf. Thank you, thank you, thank you.

As we close this part of the chapter I would like to invite you to just take a few deep breaths. Remember that everything is in Divine order and in Divine timing. Everything is exactly how it needs to be regardless of what you're feeling: the overwhelm, impatience, chaos. Switch that up to breathing in light, energy, focus, and you'll be able to calm yourself down. That's death and rebirth right there in just a few moments. It's releasing and letting go of all of these emotions that you don't need to by breathing in and rebirthing everything that you need to breathe in. This is not taboo but something that needs to be talked about. It's something that needs to be honored, loved, and embraced in such a way that it's a good thing. Should someone come to a near-death experience, that is the other side saying not time but go back and live fully, fully live.

When you've experienced that expansion of what really is out there sometimes it's hard to want to stay. But energetically and contractually it's not time.

About the Author

LEN BLEA

Len Blea was born and raised in Colorado. She is an energy reader, energy clearer, and holder of space. She channels universal energy and holds space for those during sessions. Len received her gifts at a young age but didn't know what to do with them until she became an adult and honed in on them and furthered her knowledge with them. Len has worked with men and women to focus on what is the cause of the issue and brings it to the surface and gives suggestions on how to work through it.

Len knows that part of her journey is just showing up. When someone is in need she is there. Len knows and understands that the universe brings people together as needed when needed, and for the length needed. She knows that she cannot and will not walk away from her path as it is what she is called to do.

There's not a definite word of what to say is happening during sessions and that's ok. All that matters is that Len and the client know that it is an energy flow that happens as it needs to.

Find Len here:

Email: Msmysteriousecho@gmail.com

Facebook:https://m.facebook.com/LightingLady777/?ref= bookmarks

Instagram:https://www.instagram.com/lightninglady777/ @lightninglady777

About the Publisher

HOUSE OF INDIGO

As a lifelong lover of books and all things inspirational, Jessica Verrill founded House of Indigo as a catalyst for positive impact through liberating voices and stories to facilitate healing and empowerment across the globe.

Working with leaders in the spiritual community, House of Indigo offers a high-quality, full-service product suite production of Oracle Decks, books, and companion workbooks.

For the younger generation, uplifting and inspirational children's books are a potent offering and arm of House of Indigo's publishing services.

What sets us apart is our focus on the energetic integrity of a project, high-quality production, and a focus on relationships at the core of our company.

If you are ready to share your genius through the packaging of your intellectual property, please reach out to see if we are a great fit to support you in your creations.

HouseofIndigoCollective.com